WORKS
in the Country

Contents

Introduction

There is nothing more pleasant than picnicking in the countryside on a warm summer's day. You can lie back in the grass, sniff the clear, fragrant air, listen to the hum of the busy insects and watch the fluffy cotton clouds drift overhead.

There once was a time when all the countryside was as peaceful as this, but that has changed. Man and his machines have seen to this. Even the most rural of occupations, farming, has become very mechanized, and the farmer now has to know almost as

much about machines and engines as he does about crops and livestock! Now he must use machines in order to produce enough food for us all.

The other industrial actitivies that take place in the countryside are also necessary if we want to live the way we do. There must be quarries to give us gravel and stone for building; and mines to give us the minerals we need to make metals. There must also be power stations to produce our electricity; dams and reservoirs to provide our drinking water; roads and bridges to help us travel more easily.

There is still plenty of countryside left for us to enjoy in whatever way we choose, whether it is simply hiking and camping or something more exotic like skiing and gliding.

Growing Crops

Being a farmer is one of the most important jobs in the whole world. We are very clever at making other things, but we can't make food to eat. Nature does that for us. The farmer works with nature to produce the right kinds of crops for us to eat. The farmer also raises animals to provide meat and other products. Growing crops is called arable farming. Raising animals is called livestock farming. Many farmers do both.

The Farmer's Friend

Not so long ago, if someone asked a farmer what his best friend was, he would have replied, "the cart horse." Today he would reply "the tractor." The tractor is used to pull trailers, plows and many other farm machines. It can be fitted with arms and blades and made into an excavator, ditch-digger, hedgecutter, bulldozer and power shovel.

The tractor is built not for speed, like a car, but for pulling power. It has a powerful engine which drives huge rear wheels. The wheels carry massive tires with chunky treads so that they grip the ground well. The front wheels are usually very much smaller and closer together.

The tractor usually has a diesel engine, like a truck. Then it uses oil as a fuel. Some tractor engines, however, run on gasoline like a car engine. Others burn kerosene (paraffin) or liquid gas.

The tractor works and is driven in much the same way as a car or truck, through a clutch, propellershaft and gearbox. Often it has power steering to make it easier to drive. Power steering uses part of the engine power to steer the front wheels. This prevents the driver getting too tired when the tractor is moving over heavy ground.

If the ground gets too heavy and waterlogged, the farmer may have to use a caterpillar, or crawler tractor instead. This has twin tracks of steel plates instead of wheels. The tracks

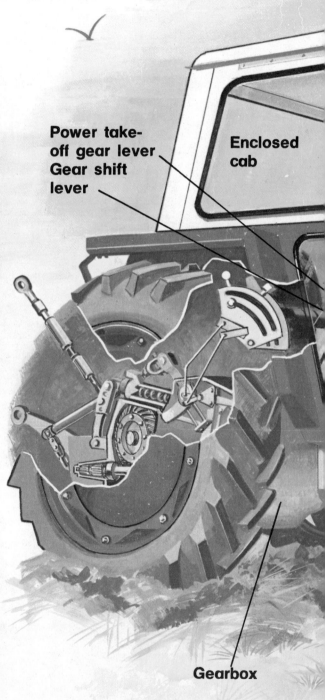

Power take-off gear lever
Gear shift lever

Enclosed cab

Gearbox

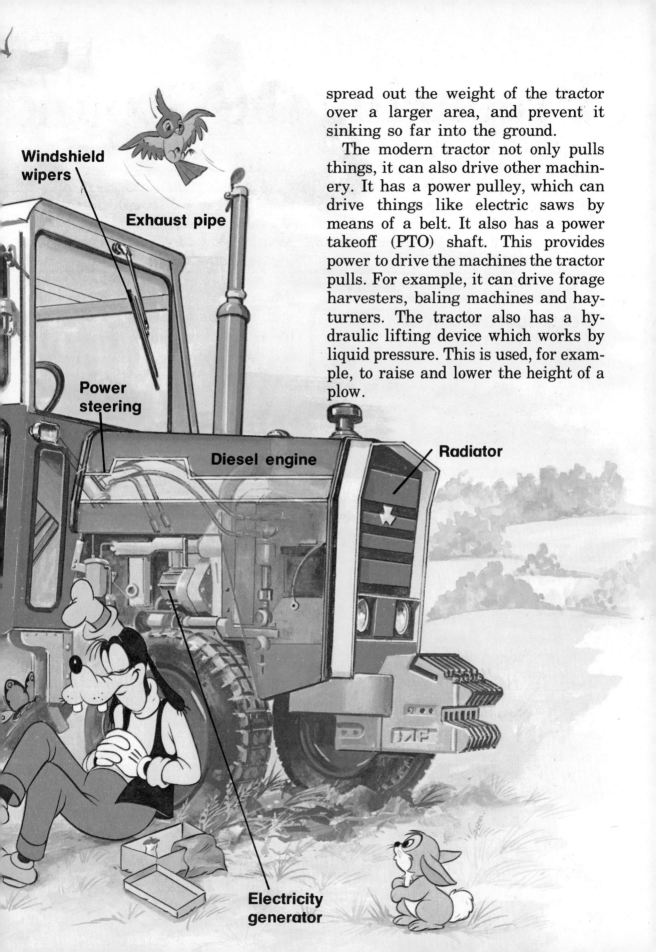

Windshield wipers

Exhaust pipe

Power steering

Diesel engine

Radiator

Electricity generator

spread out the weight of the tractor over a larger area, and prevent it sinking so far into the ground.

The modern tractor not only pulls things, it can also drive other machinery. It has a power pulley, which can drive things like electric saws by means of a belt. It also has a power takeoff (PTO) shaft. This provides power to drive the machines the tractor pulls. For example, it can drive forage harvesters, baling machines and hayturners. The tractor also has a hydraulic lifting device which works by liquid pressure. This is used, for example, to raise and lower the height of a plow.

Preparing the Ground

Crops cannot be grown successfully on any piece of land. They must be grown on ground that has been well looked after and suitably prepared to receive the seeds or young plants. The farmer prepares, or tills, the ground in several stages. First he plows it, then he harrows it and often he rolls it too.

The plow was one of the greatest of all man's inventions for it enabled him to become a farmer and start to lead a more settled way of life. Early plows were made of wood and pulled by hand. Modern plows are made of tough steel and pulled by tractor. Plowing is useful for many reasons. It breaks up hard ground and leaves the soil in ridges with furrows in between. The action of the air and the weather on the exposed soil helps break it up more and make it

Four-furrow plow

Moldboard Plowshare Cutting discs

"sweeter." By turning over the soil, plowing also buries and kills the surface weeds.

The main parts of a plow are the curved blades, which turn over thick "slices" of soil as they cut through the ground. The part of the blade in front at the bottom is known as the share. It is sharp-edged and designed to slice the soil from underneath. The main part of the plow blade is called the moldboard. In front of each blade is a sharp disc, or coulter, which cuts into the ground vertically and feeds a slice of soil to the blade.

A plow is described by the number of furrows it makes. Four- and five-furrow plows are quite common these days. Some plows are simply drawn by the tractor and are supported by wheels. Others are mounted on the rear of the tractor and are raised and lowered hydraulically.

After plowing the farmer needs to smooth down the ridges and break up the large clods of soil. He does this by harrowing. There are several kinds of harrows. The disc harrow consists of several sets of sharp discs, which rotate as they are pulled through the ground. Other kinds of harrows have chains or spiked teeth to break up the soil.

Disc harrow

Main frame

Scalloped discs

Plain discs

Sowing and Planting

"We plow the fields and scatter the good seed on the land," goes the popular hymn, but scattering the seed over the land is a very haphazard and wasteful way of sowing, so most farmers sow their seeds with a drill. A seed drill sows the seeds in rows beneath the ground at the correct depth and in carefully measured quantities. Because the seed is buried, the birds cannot get at it so easily. Seed drills are used to sow many crops.

Seed is sown on land that has recently been harrowed and possibly rolled. The seed drill is pulled by a tractor. The seed is carried in a box, or hopper. At the bottom of the hopper is a wheel or roller that feeds a steady supply of seeds into a row of delivery tubes. The tubes carry the seeds down into the ground. The seeds drop into shallow furrows made by sharp, rotating discs (coulters) or spikes. Attached to the rear of the drill are harrows, which move the soil back into the furrows to cover up the seeds.

Farmers often apply fertilizers to the land either before or during drilling. By applying fertilizers, they put back into the ground substances that growing plants take out, such as nitrogen and phosphorus. They get better crops as a result. They also apply chalk or lime to the soil to make it less acid. Farmyard manure is an excellent fertilizer. It is a mixture of animal waste and rotted straw. There is not enough manure available for all the farmer's needs, however, so he has to use chemical fertilizers as well.

Before drilling, farmers apply fertilizers with various spreading devices. A common one consists of a hopper that drops the fertilizer on to rotating discs, which scatter it over the ground. During drilling fertilizer is delivered into the furrows with the seeds from a separate hopper.

Farmers also use machinery for planting other crops, such as potatoes, cabbages and tomatoes. Many of these machines have to be fed by hand.

Seed drill

Coulters

Seed Hopper

Harrow

Spikes

Spraying the Crops

A farmer cannot simply forget about his crops once they have been planted. They must be looked after and protected all the time until they are ready for harvesting. Otherwise they will be attacked by disease, pests and weeds.

Disease is usually the worst enemy. All kinds of funguses, molds, mildews and viruses can attack crops and even completely wipe them out. Insect pests can also create havoc – including many kinds of aphids, flies, caterpillars, beetles and weevils. Weeds cause trouble because they are tougher and often grow faster than the planted crop and can soon smother it, so the farmer can end up with a fine crop of weeds!

Farmers use chemicals to prevent attack or reduce its effect. They use fungicides against fungus diseases, and insecticides against insect pests. Against weeds they use selective weed-killers, or herbicides, which kill the weeds without harming the crop.

Spray boom

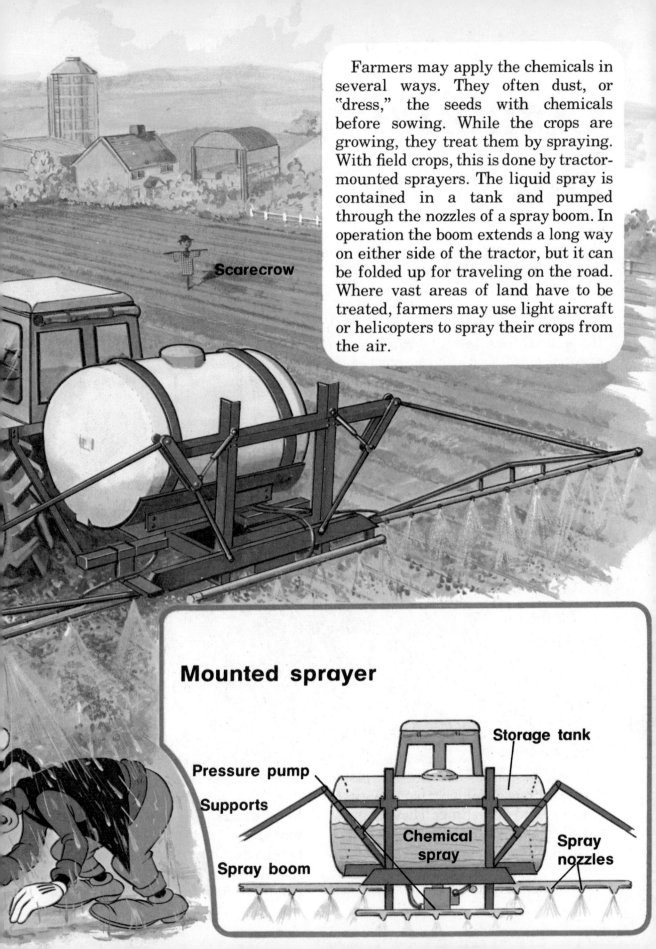

Farmers may apply the chemicals in several ways. They often dust, or "dress," the seeds with chemicals before sowing. While the crops are growing, they treat them by spraying. With field crops, this is done by tractor-mounted sprayers. The liquid spray is contained in a tank and pumped through the nozzles of a spray boom. In operation the boom extends a long way on either side of the tractor, but it can be folded up for traveling on the road. Where vast areas of land have to be treated, farmers may use light aircraft or helicopters to spray their crops from the air.

Scarecrow

Mounted sprayer

Storage tank

Pressure pump

Supports

Chemical spray

Spray nozzles

Spray boom

Combine Harvester

Steering wheel

Cutter controls

Grain hopper

Beaters

Threshing drum

Elevator

Reel

Dividers

Cutting bar

Fa

These days only a few people work on the land as farmers, but they have to produce enough food for everybody. They can do this only with the help of machines, such as tractors, plows, drills and combine harvesters. With these machines farmers can prepare ground, plant seeds and harvest crops much faster than they once could.

The combine harvester is one of the largest and most useful of their machines. They use combines to harvest cereals such as wheat, barley, rye and rice. They also use them to harvest other crops, including beans and peas.

Combine harvesters are so called because they combine the actions of reaping and threshing. They reap, or cut the crop; then they thresh it, or separate the grain from the straw and chaff.

Most modern combines, like the one shown here, have their own engine; they are self-propelled. Earlier ones were drawn by tractors. Large combines can cut a swathe (width) of twenty feet (over six meters). The vast wheatfields on the prairies of North America are harvested by teams of

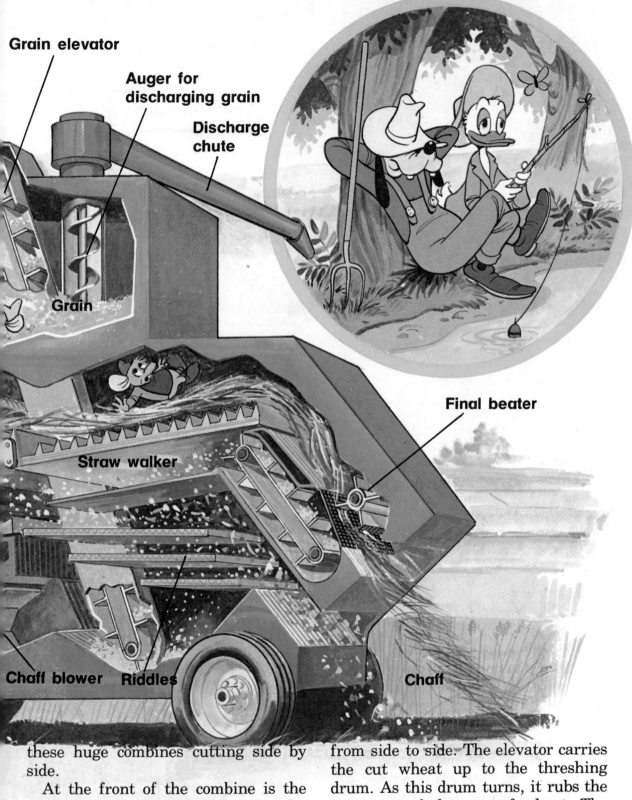

Grain elevator

Auger for
discharging grain

Discharge
chute

Grain

Final beater

Straw walker

Chaff blower   Riddles

Chaff

these huge combines cutting side by side.

At the front of the combine is the reel. This turns around and pushes the wheat on to the cutter bar and elevator. The cutter bar has a razor-sharp knife blade, which cuts as it moves rapidly from side to side. The elevator carries the cut wheat up to the threshing drum. As this drum turns, it rubs the grain out of the ears of wheat. The grain and chaff fall through the bars of the concave riddle, while the straw carries on to the straw walker.

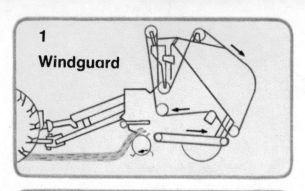

1 Windguard

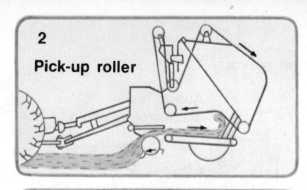

2 Pick-up roller

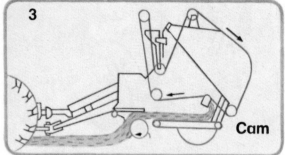

3 Cam

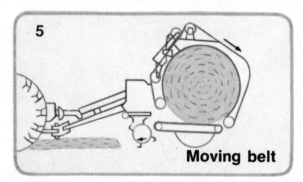

4 Moving belt

5 Moving belt

6 Tractor

Making Hay

Cereals such as barley and wheat are often the main crops grown on a farm, but grass is an important crop too. We do not usually think of grass as a crop, but it is a vital forage crop – one that is grown to feed sheep and cattle.

These animals can graze on the grass for much of the year, but in winter the grass stops growing. Then the animals must be fed on other foods. One of the cheapest of these is hay, which is dried grass. Farmers cut and dry the grass in the late spring or early summer when it is growing vigorously. They often harvest two crops of hay a year.

They do not usually grow grass in the same fields year after year, but grow it in rotation with other crops. They often grow grass in a field that has been used for cereals. Rotating the crops in this way helps to keep the soil healthy and productive.

During haymaking the farmer cuts the grass with tractor-drawn mowers, and then leaves it on the ground to dry into hay. He rakes it into long rows with mechanical rakes, which consist of rotating wire wheels with prongs at the end. He turns the rows over periodically until the hay is thoroughly dry. Then it can be safely gathered without rotting.

Sometimes the farmer uses an ordinary baling machine to pick up the hay. The machine picks it up, compresses it with a powerful plunger, and then ties it in oblong bales.

A more modern hay collector produces large rolls of hay, not bales. This is shown in the picture. The small series of diagrams shows how it works. A rotating pick-up roller lifts the hay from the ground on to a moving belt. It travels to the rear of the machine where it comes into contact with another moving belt. This belt sends the hay around in a circle, and a roll of hay begins to form. This gets bigger until it is big enough to be ejected from the back of the machine.

Hay collector

Pick-up roller

Making Silage

Making hay is not the only way of storing grass for winter animal feed. Grass can also be stored as silage. It is cut early in the year when it is at its juiciest and then stored in a tower called a silo. While it is stored, it ferments but keeps its food value and remains juicy. Cattle fed on silage keep as healthy and produce nearly as much milk as they do when grazing grass.

Grass for silage is cut with a forage harvester, which is pulled and powered by a tractor. This machine cuts and chops up the grass into small pieces with a rotating flail, and then blows it through a curved overhead chute into a trailer. The trailer may form part of the harvester or be separate, pulled by another tractor.

The cut, chopped grass is then blown into the silo, which is then sealed tightly so that air cannot get in. The grass then gradually ferments, producing acid which helps preserve it. Sometimes extra acid is added to help the process.

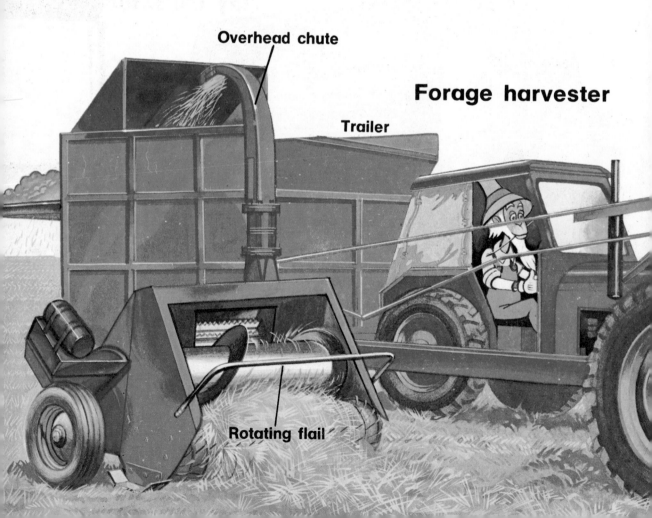

Overhead chute

Forage harvester

Trailer

Rotating flail

Modern silos are metal towers 50 feet (15 meters) or more in height and 18 feet (5 meters) or more in diameter. They are usually fitted with equipment that delivers the mature silage from the bottom of the silo into trailers or directly into feeding troughs. Some silos are made of concrete or wood. Others simply consist of trenches covered over with plastic sheeting.

Grass is by no means the only crop used for silage. Clover and alfalfa are also widely used. They are doubly valuable to the farmer because they enrich the soil with nitrogen as they grow. Green cereals such as rye, oats and maize (corn) are also often used as silage in some countries.

Forage silo

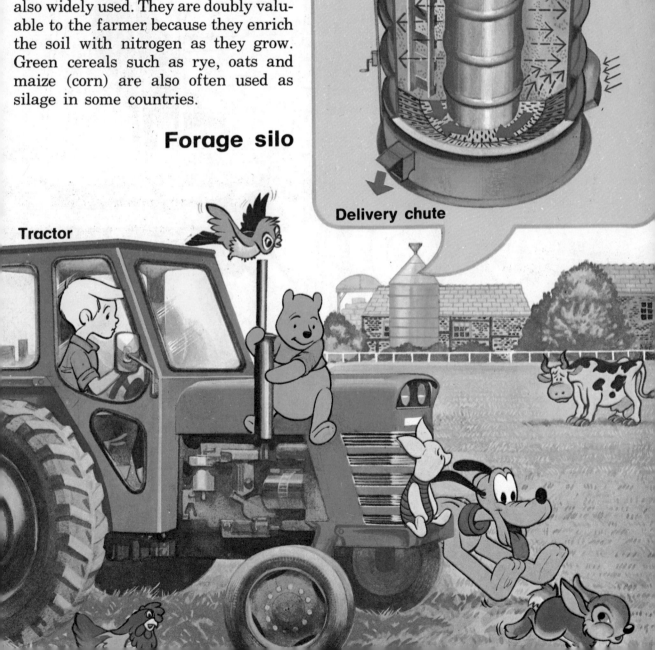

Fermenting grass

Delivery chute

Tractor

Harvesting Roots

Farmers also grow various root crops to feed their animals during the winter, including turnips, rutabaga and fodder beets. They also grow other crops to sell. The most important of these are

Automatic potato harvester

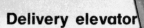
Moving belt

Delivery elevator

Tractor

Depth control unit

Rollers

Plowshare

Hydraulic height control

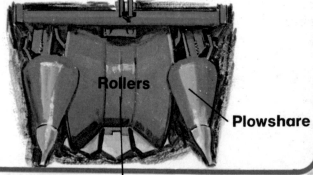

drum elevator — Separator control lever

Separator

Rubber-spined belt **Separator**

Elevator drum

"Trailer"

Manual potato harvester

sugar beets and potatoes. Sugar beets are so called because sugar can be obtained from them. Sugar beets are our most important source of sugar after sugar cane.

Potatoes are usually classed as a root crop because they grow in the ground. In fact they are not roots but enlarged stems, or tubers. Baked, boiled or fried, they are one of our most important vegetables. They came originally from South America and were introduced to Europe by the Spaniards in the 1500s.

Harvesting of the root crops is now usually done by machines. Among the most interesting of these are the potato harvesters. Some simply dig up the potatoes and leave them on the ground to be picked up by hand. Others dig up the potatoes, separate them from the dirt, and deliver them into a trailer. One of these automatic machines is shown here.

The potato harvester is drawn by a tractor and in front has a digging blade, or share, which scoops up the potatoes and dirt and delivers them on to an elevator. The elevator is made up of an endless belt with slats across it. A lot of the dirt falls through the slats as the elevator carries the potatoes to a circular drum elevator at the rear of the machine. This elevator in turn carries the potatoes to the separator. In the separator the potatoes fall on to another moving belt, while any remaining dirt and stones are removed by a rubber-spined belt and discharged at the rear. The potatoes meanwhile travel to the delivery elevator, which is angled so as to deliver them into a trailer moving alongside. The pictures show the problems you have when you forget the trailer!

Fruitful Labor

Nature provides us with all kinds of delicious fruits.

As with all crops, certain fruits grow best in certain climates. Apples and pears, for example, prefer a moist temperate climate, which is not too hot and not too cold. Citrus fruits, such as oranges and lemons, prefer a much warmer, drier climate. Fruits such as mangoes thrive only in hot and humid tropical climates. These days, thanks to modern methods of transport and refrigeration, we can enjoy not only fruits grown locally in their natural season, but also fruits from countries throughout the world.

Most ripe fruits are relatively soft compared with most other crops, and easily damaged. If they do get damaged, they quickly rot. For this reason they are usually harvested by hand rather than by machines. Hand picking is relatively slow and is also increasingly expensive, but it will probably always be necessary for soft fruits.

Machinery is, however, coming into use for harvesting some of the "harder" fruits. Apples and plums are sometimes picked with the help of mechanical tree shakers. These machines shake the tree and collect the falling fruit in large canvas-covered "wings."

The new type of apple picker shown here gives much better results. The apple trees are grown in a special way so that they form a flat "wall," rather than spreading on all sides as they normally do. The machine then straddles the wall when harvesting. It is made up of two conveyors angled upward. The conveyors carry sets of prongs, or "picking fingers," which are plastic rods covered in foam rubber. The fingers pluck the apples from the fruit wall as they move continuously up and around. The picked apples roll on to an elevator, which carries them to the rear of the machine be boxed.

Manual apple shaker

Corn and Cotton

Sweet corn, popcorn, cornflakes and cornstarch all come from different varieties of one of the most important food crops in the world – corn. Like wheat, corn is a cereal, and it is second only to wheat in the area of farmland planted. The United States produces half of the world's supply of corn, which is called maize in some parts of the world.

Corn is used as a forage crop for animals as well as a food crop. It can be grazed when recently sown and can also be made into silage (page 23).

Corn grows up to 10 feet (3 meters) tall. It has a thick stem, from which large leaves shoot at intervals. The grain is produced in ears, which grow from the joints between leaf and stem. The ears consist of grain tightly packed around a woody cob. They are wrapped in overlapping leaves, or husks. A corn plant may produce as many as eight ears.

Various machines are used to harvest a corn crop. Some (pickers) simply snap the ears from the stalks. Some (picker-huskers) pick the ears and remove the husks by means of rotating rollers. Others (picker-shellers) shell the ears as well, ejecting the cobs into a trailer.

Manual cotton picker

Corn plants

Cutters

28

The United States is also the world's biggest producer of cotton, which is grown mainly in the hot southern states. The cotton plant is quite a small shrub, which produces its seeds in bolls. When ripe, the boll bursts open to expose a fluffy mass of cotton fibers, which cover the seed.

A great deal of cotton is still picked by hand in many countries, but in the United States, cotton picking is mechanized. The machines ride high off the ground over the cotton plants, stripping off the outer parts of the plant with revolving rollers or steel fingers, picking not only the bolls but twigs and leaves as well. Picking machines do a much better job. They have rotating spindles that pick the cotton from the open bolls, but leave unripe bolls untouched. The picked cotton is then delivered to a large collecting basket on top of the picker.

Corn picker

Discharge chute

Cob collector

As well as growing crops, the farmer raises animals to provide food and for other reasons. The animals he raises are called livestock. He improves the quality of his livestock by selective breeding, or breeding from only his best animals.

The most important livestock are cattle, sheep, pigs and poultry. Cattle provide us with the meat we call beef. Female cattle, cows, give us milk as well. Sheep provide us with the meats mutton and lamb; pigs, with the fresh meat pork and with the cured meats bacon and ham. Poultry provide us with eggs as well as meat. Livestock also give us other useful things, such as leather and wool.

In some parts of the world livestock such as horses, mules and buffaloes are still used as draft animals to draw, or pull, plows and other implements. They may also be used as pack animals to carry loads.

SALE
OF
PRIZE
BULLS

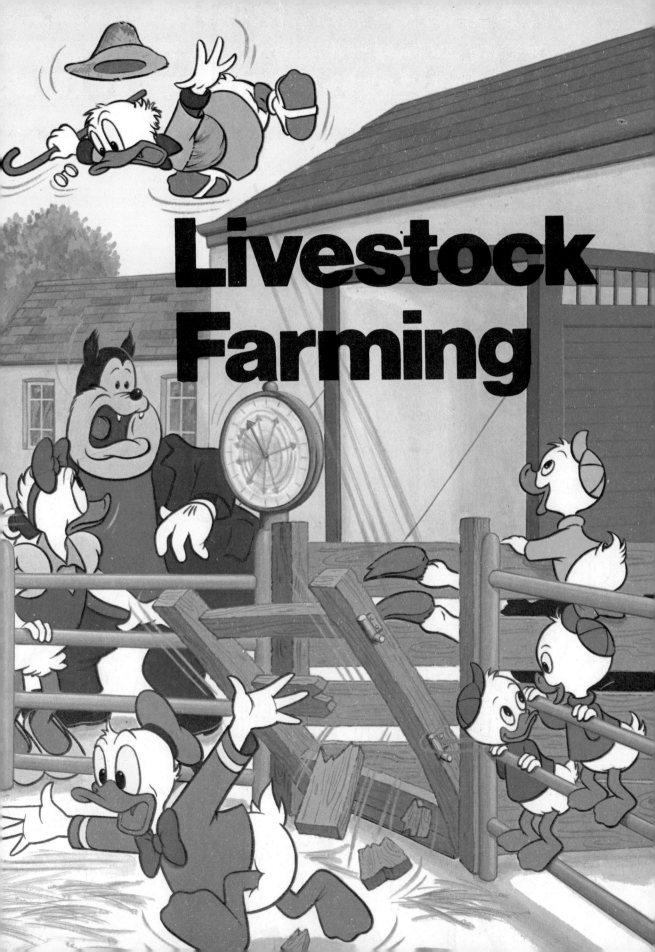

Livestock Farming

Milking in the Parlor

Cows' milk is one of the most nourishing foods there is. We not only drink it, but also make it into butter and cheese. To produce the vast amount of milk we

need, farmers keep large herds of dairy cows, which they must milk morning and evening. To make this possible, almost all milking is now done by machines.

On most dairy farms now the cows are milked in specially designed milking parlors. The cows enter separate stalls where they can be penned in and supplied with fodder to eat while they are being milked. Each stall is fitted with suction equipment for milking. This consists of metal cups attached by rubber tubing to a suction pump. The cups fit over the teats on the cow's udder, and the suction draws off the milk and delivers it into a recording jar. A separate jar is used for each cow, and a record is kept of its daily milk yield. Afterward the milk goes through a milk cooler which helps prevent it spoiling. From there it is pumped into a tanker for delivery to the dairy, which will pasteurize it to kill germs and then bottle it or make it into dairy products.

The most modern dairy farms often use a rotary milking parlor like the one you see in the picture. It is made up of mány stalls arranged in a circle on a rotating turntable. The cows enter and leave the stalls one by one as the turntable rotates. Once they are in a stall the breast rail at the front and the rump rail behind keep them penned in. Fodder is placed in the manger in the middle for them to feed on. Milking proceeds while the turntable turns.

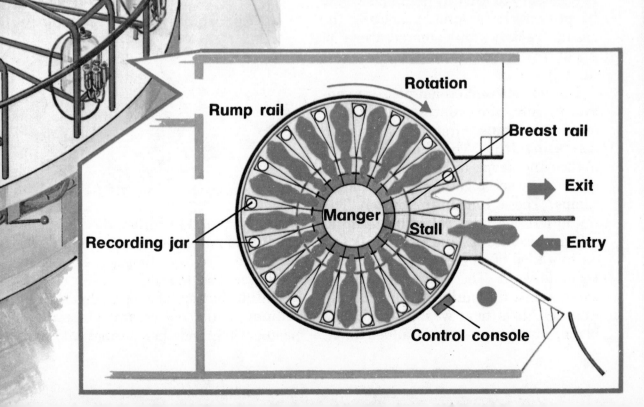

Rotation

Rump rail

Breast rail

Exit

Entry

Manger

Stall

Recording jar

Control console

Butter and Cheese

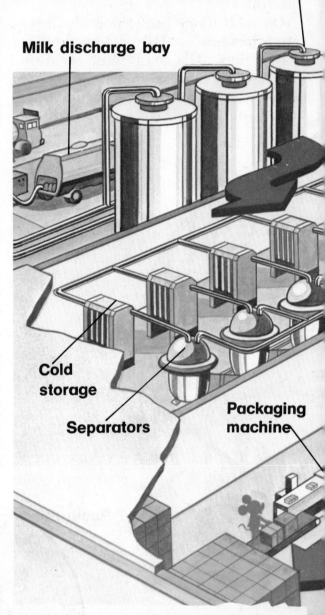

Milk is delicious to drink and is one of the most important of all our foods. It is also valuable because it can be made into two other nourishing foods: butter and cheese.

Butter is made in factories called creameries. The picture shows a very modern one in which machines make butter continuously and largely automatically. The milk arrives from the dairy farms in huge tankers and is pumped into storage tanks, or silos. From these it is pumped in turn into the separators.

In the separators the cream is removed from the milk because butter is made from the cream alone. Usually the separators are machines called centrifuges, which whirl round and round rather like a spin drier. The cream must then be pasteurized. This process is necessary to kill any germs that may be present. It is done by heating the cream rapidly to a temperature of about 167°F (75°C) and then cooling it quickly.

The pasteurized cream passes eventually into the continuous butter-making machine. First it is churned in a rotating drum. The churning action makes the drops of fat in the cream gradually come together to form larger lumps. These lumps are butter. The liquid left behind is called buttermilk.

The butter lumps and buttermilk fall on to a kind of conveyor which pushes them forward. The buttermilk drains away, while the butter is continuously kneaded. It is next washed, and then brine, or salty water, is added to it.

After further kneading, the butter is ready and comes out of the machine as an endless yellow "tongue." It is then packaged and boxed.

Unlike butter, cheese is made from ordinary milk, not cream. The milk is pasteurized, and then rennet and acid

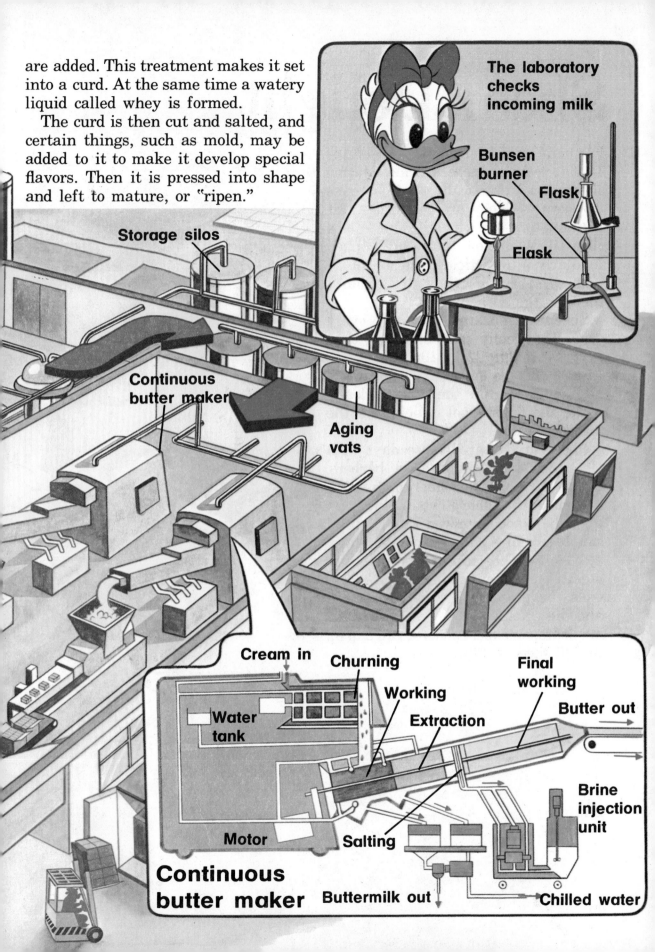

are added. This treatment makes it set into a curd. At the same time a watery liquid called whey is formed.

The curd is then cut and salted, and certain things, such as mold, may be added to it to make it develop special flavors. Then it is pressed into shape and left to mature, or "ripen."

The laboratory checks incoming milk

Bunsen burner

Flask

Flask

Storage silos

Continuous butter maker

Aging vats

Continuous butter maker

Cream in

Churning

Working

Final working

Butter out

Water tank

Extraction

Motor

Salting

Brine injection unit

Buttermilk out

Chilled water

Shear Delight

Farmers have been raising sheep for 10,000 years or more. On most farms sheep spend practically all their lives in pastures. They are rounded up at lambing time and when they have to be sheared or dipped. They are dipped regularly in insecticide solution to rid them of parasites that would harm them or their wool.

Sheep are sheared regularly every year. The woolly coat, or fleece, they grow can weigh 22 lb (10 kg) or more. English breeds such as the Cotswold and Romney grow the longest fleece, while the finest wool comes from the Merino breeds.

Sheep are sheared these days with electric shears, rather like barbers' clippers. They have a steel comb at the bottom, with a sharp cutting blade on top. The blade is moved rapidly from side to side by a pronged fork driven by electricity. The cutter is adjusted by means of the tension nut, which controls the pressure between the comb and the cutting blade. Using this type of shears, an expert shearer can clip up to 200 sheep a day.

Shearing machine

Clipping shears

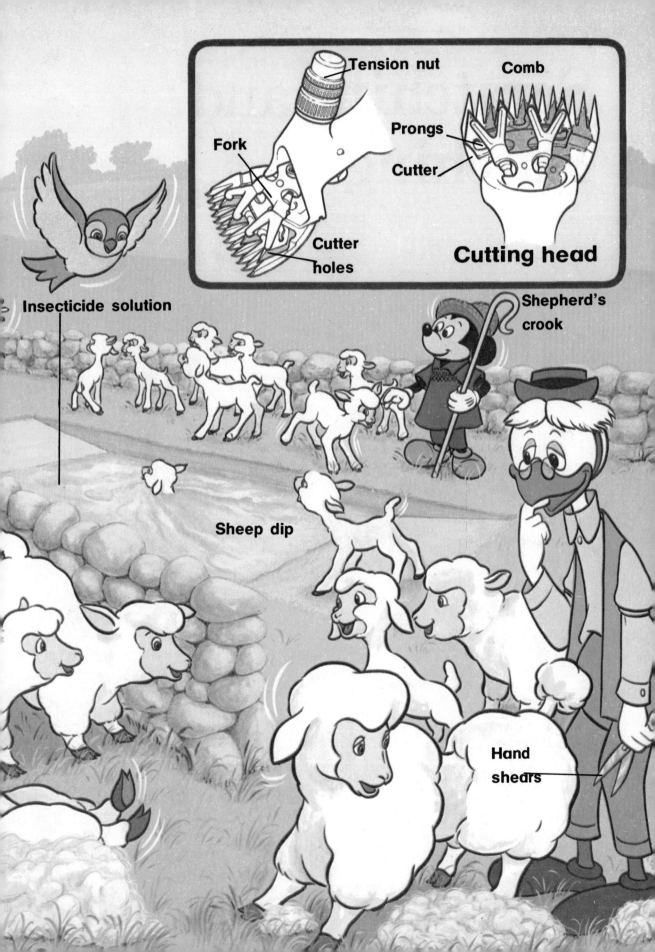

Tension nut

Comb

Fork

Prongs

Cutter

Cutter holes

Cutting head

Insecticide solution

Shepherd's crook

Sheep dip

Hand shears

Scratching and Hatching

Cabinet incubator

Hen battery

Bulb

Simple incubator

Rooster

Down on the farm some of the pleasantest sounds are the crowing of roosters in the morning and the clucking of the hens after they have laid their eggs.

Chickens are the most important kind of poultry raised on farms. They are descended from jungle fowl, which still exist in the wild parts of southern Asia. Turkeys, ducks and geese are other poultry raised in very large numbers, but on nowhere the same scale as chickens. Something like 4,000 million chickens are raised every year throughout the world.

Ordinary farmyard hens breed by first mating with a rooster, then laying and sitting on the fertilized eggs until they hatch. These hens are called brood hens. In the warmth provided by the hen's body, the chicks start to grow inside the eggs. In three weeks they are ready to peck their way out of the shells.

This natural method is not convenient for large-scale chicken farming, and so farmers hatch the fertilized eggs in incubators. In an incubator the eggs are kept under conditions similar to those under a brood hen. They are kept at a temperature of about 100°F (38°C) (blood heat) and in a rather humid (moist) atmosphere. Warm air is blown over the eggs which are held in trays. The eggs are turned automatically from time to time so that they are warmed evenly all over. Some incubators can hold tens of thousands of eggs at once.

Once they have hatched, the chicks are kept in electrically heated brooder houses until they are about two months old. Those raised for meat are then moved to large broiler houses and fed concentrated food under carefully controlled conditions. In only about ten weeks they reach a weight of over 4 lb (1.8 kg) and are ready for the market. Egg-laying pullets (young hens) start laying at about six months old. They may be kept in large houses provided with laying boxes, or in individual wire cages, or batteries.

Wood frame
Bitumen lining
Cork insulation
Steel casing

Automatic turning gear

Free-range hens

Brood hen

39

Battery-operated unit

Four 9-volt batteries

Circuit board

Insulated support

Electric fencing

Pig Farming

Millions upon millions of pigs are raised each year throughout the world. Brazil raises the most pigs – over 60 million of them! Pigs are useful animals on a farm for they do not take up much room; they can easily be fed on surplus crops, and they fatten quickly.

Unlike most farmyard animals, pigs do not have thick fur or hair and they must be allowed to shelter at night and in the winter. They are often kept in low sheds called sties, provided with plenty of straw, and have a pen outside for exercise. On big modern pig farms, however, large numbers of pigs are housed inside all the time in large air-conditioned barns. The temperature is carefully controlled and the pigs are fed just the right food. In these conditions the pigs fatten very quickly indeed, and are ready for market in under six months.

Pigs also breed very easily and quickly. Sows, female pigs, give birth to their young after 114 days. They often produce eight or more piglets in each litter. As with all young livestock, the piglets must be particularly well looked after for the first few weeks of their lives. If the farmer thinks anything is wrong, he calls in the vet, or veterinary surgeon, to take a look at them.

During the summer months farmers often let their pigs loose in the fields, giving them simple wooden huts to sleep in. They often keep them in by means of an electric fence. This is a bare-wire fence through which electricity from a battery is passed. If the pig touches the wire, it receives a small electric shock.

Power

Insulators

Electricity substation

42

One thing most of us take for granted these days is electricity. When you press the light switch, you expect the light to come on. Where does this electricity come from? The chances are that it comes from a long way away. It is carried to our homes through cables from a distant power station. This station may use steam or flowing water to spin the turbogenerators which produce the electricity.

Electricity is the most useful form of power we have, for it can be sent, or transmitted, over long distances without much loss. It saves us each having to produce our own electricity at home.

Power cables

Blowing in the Wind

Not so very long ago there was no electricity and no gasoline or diesel engines to provide people with the power to drive machines. They had to use either animals or sources of power that exist in nature. The natural sources they used first were the wind and flowing water (page 46).

Man has harnessed the wind from very early times. He first harnessed it by hoisting sails to propel his boats, but it was not until about 1,100 years ago that he began using the wind to drive machinery. He did so by building windmills. They were so called because they were used to mill, or grind grain into flour.

Windmills remained in widespread use throughout the world until the beginning of this century, but were then gradually replaced by more efficient equipment. Some mills have now been restored and are in working order once again. They are fascinating places to visit. In some countries windmills were also built to pump water from the land. This happened particularly in the Netherlands, where windmills are a familiar part of the landscape.

A typical windmill has a round tower built of wood or brick. On top of the tower is a turret, which holds the cross-shaped sails that catch the wind. The sails turn around in a more or less vertical, or upright plane. Usually their blades are made up of wooden slats set at an angle. As the sails rotate, they turn the shafts and gears

Fantail

Sails

Turret

Tower

44

Slats

Spider

Fantail

Bell cranks

Wind shaft

Iron worm

Brake band

Shutter bar

Brake shaft

Spur wheel

Millstones

that spin the millstone which grinds the grain.

The turret is free to turn around the tower so that the sails can always face into the wind. To make this happen, a small bladed wheel called the fantail is mounted on the turret on the opposite side from the sails. Whichever way the wind blows, the fantail always positions itself downwind. It is an automatic control device.

In some parts of the world modern windmills called wind turbines are found. They are used at isolated farms, for example, to produce electricity and for pumping. They are tall steel towers with a bladed wheel on top, which turns in the wind. They are coupled to a small electric generator to produce electricity. Giant wind turbines are now also developed to help solve the world's energy shortage.

45

Rushing Water

You only have to see a swollen mountain stream to realize how much power there is in swift-flowing water. The Romans appreciated this over 2,000 years ago and were probably the first to build waterwheels. Like windmills, waterwheels were first used to grind grain into flour. Later they were used to power machines, such as tilthammers for metal working. Some watermills are still working. The modern version of the waterwheel – the water turbine – is now widely used to produce electricity in hydroelectric power stations (see page 48).

Waterwheels are not usually sited in the main stream of water, but nearby, and a narrow channel is cut to divert water to the wheel. Channeled in this way, the water flows more swiftly and has more power to turn the wheel. The traditional kind of waterwheel is usually made of wood and has many blades around its edge. It can be as tall as a house.

The water may be channeled underneath the wheel; then it is called an undershot wheel. Or it may be channeled over the wheel, when it is called an overshot wheel. In this type, the weight of the water in the bucket-like vanes falling from a height causes the wheel to spin. It is much more efficient than the undershot type.

The diagram of the gear arrangements shows one way in which a water

wheel can be used to drive the millstones. At the other end of the shaft from the wheel is a large gearwheel, called the pit wheel because it is let into the floor. This turns the main drive shaft through a right-angled gear. A large gear called the spur wheel turns another shaft that spins

Mill race

one of the millstones. There is a hole in the upper millstone (runner stone) to run in the grain. Another large gear (crown wheel) at the top of the drive shaft powers other equipment used in the mill. It turns a horizontal shaft, from which power is taken by drive belts.

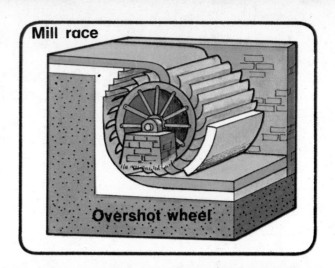

Mill race

Overshot wheel

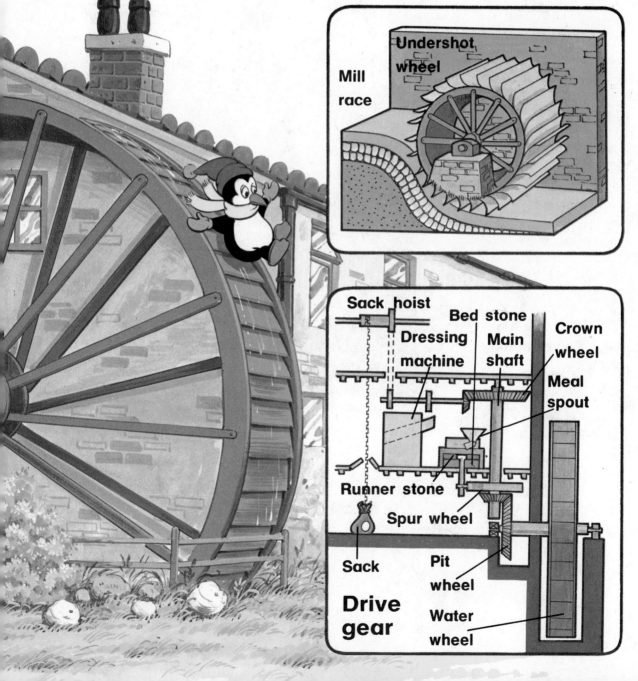

Mill race

Undershot wheel

Sack hoist

Bed stone

Main shaft

Crown wheel

Dressing machine

Meal spout

Runner stone

Spur wheel

Sack

Pit wheel

Drive gear

Water wheel

Hydroelectricity

Dam

Power house

Shaft to generator

Water inlet

Runner

Guide vanes

Runner vanes

Water outlet

In many mountainous parts of the world the power in running water is harnessed to produce electricity. This is done at hydroelectric ("water-electric") power stations. At these stations water is passed through water turbines and spins them round. They are modern kinds of waterwheel.

The turbines are connected to generators, which are machines that generate, or produce electricity when they spin. Each turbine and coupled generator make up what is called a turbogenerator set. The powerhouse of a dam contains several turbogenerator sets.

The water for the turbines is taken from a high-level lake. It gains energy as it falls to a lower level, and it is this energy which spins the turbines. Sometimes a natural lake, or reservoir has

to be made. This is done by building a barrier called a dam across a river valley. The water builds up behind the dam, flooding the valley.

There are several kinds of dams – some built of concrete, others of rocks, clay and soil. As water becomes deeper, it exerts greater and greater pressure, so dams must be very solidly built. Some dams stand up to the pressure because they are very bulky. They contain millions upon millions of cubic feet of concrete or rock. They are called gravity dams. They are usually straight and have a cross-section like a triangle. They are widest at the bottom, where the water pressure is highest.

Another kind of dam has the shape of an arch or dome. It gets its strength from its shape, not from its weight.

Full Steam Ahead

Two out of every three power stations use steam turbines rather than water turbines to spin the electricity generators. In most power stations the steam is produced, or "raised" in boilers heated by burning coal or oil. In a few stations nuclear reactors are used to produce the heat needed to turn water mto steam (page 52).

The steam produced in the boilers is channeled to the steam turbines at very high temperature (over 900°F or 500°C) and at very high pressure (over 300 times atmospheric pressure). The steam turbine consists of a number of bladed wheels mounted on a shaft. This shaft is coupled to the electricity generator. The steam passes from one turbine wheel to the other, spinning them as it does so. It is directed on to each wheel at the right angle by guide vanes fixed to the turbine casing.

The main picture shows a coal-fired steam power station. Coal from a hopper passes into a machine called the pulverizer, which grinds it into dust. It is then blown along by a current of hot air into the furnace, where it is burned. Running through the furnace are tubes containing the boiler water. The water turns to steam and is piped into the turbine.

After it has passed through the turbine, the steam enters the condenser. The condenser contains tubes through which cold water flows. The steam is cooled and condenses, or changes back into water. This is then pumped back into the boiler. The cooling water gets hot as it passes through the condenser and must in turn be cooled. This is often done in a cooling tower. This is a huge cone-shaped tower down which the warm water is allowed to trickle. As it does so, some water evaporates. This cools the remaining water, in just the same way as perspiring on a hot day cools your skin.

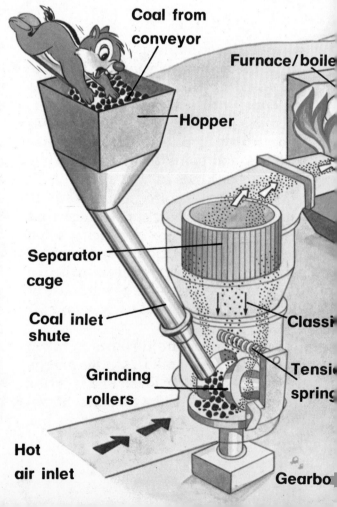

Coal from conveyor

Furnace/boile

Hopper

Separator cage

Coal inlet shute

Classi

Tensi spring

Grinding rollers

Hot air inlet

Gearbo

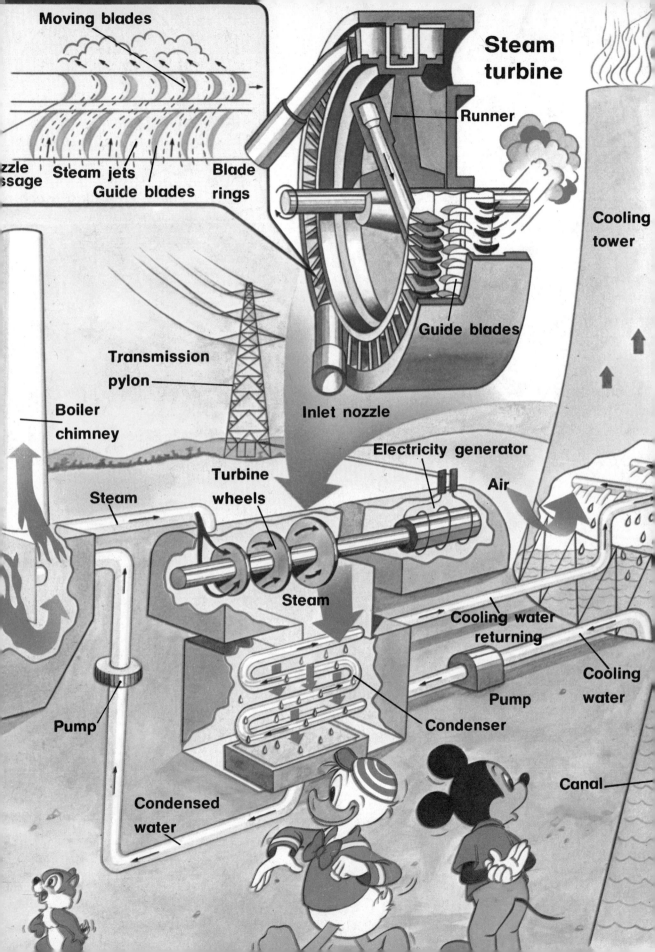

Moving blades

Steam turbine

zzle
ssage

Steam jets

Guide blades

Blade rings

Runner

Cooling tower

Guide blades

Transmission pylon

Boiler chimney

Inlet nozzle

Electricity generator

Air

Steam

Turbine wheels

Steam

Cooling water returning

Cooling water

Pump

Pump

Condenser

Canal

Condensed water

Fueling machine

Computer room

Heating and ventilating plant

Maintenance area

Turbine unit maintenance crane

Visitors' viewing balcony

Turbogenerator

Fuel disposal chute

Cooling pool

Fueling pipes

Concret reactor vessel

Evaporator plant

Loading bay

Power from the Atom

Locked inside every atom, or minute particle, of matter is a tremendous amount of power. Certain atoms can be split in order to release this power, which can be turned into electricity. We call the splitting of atoms "fission," and the power produced "atomic," or "nuclear" power. Britain, the United States, Russia, France and several other countries now get quite a lot of electricity from nuclear power stations.

The main part of a nuclear power station is the reactor. Inside the reactor there are cans containing pellets of uranium. Uranium is a metal whose atoms can be made to split easily. When the uranium atoms split, a lot of energy is given out as heat. A gas or liquid passes through the reactor and carries away the heat.

The hot gas or liquid passes through pipes in a heat exchanger, which con-tains water. The water is heated to boiling point and turns into steam. The steam is then piped into ordinary steam turbines and spins them round. The turbines are connected to generators, which produce electricity.

When uranium atoms split, a lot of dangerous rays are given off as well as heat, so the reactor is built inside a thick concrete and steel container. This shields the people operating the power station from the rays. There are many safety devices in the reactor to prevent it becoming overheated. The tempera-ture is controlled by means of control rods. If it rises too much, the control rods are pushed further into the reac-tor and slow down the atom-splitting process. If anything else goes wrong in the reactor, the control rods go right in and shut the reactor down; so whatever happens, a reactor can never blow up.

Model of a nuclear power station

Nuclear reactor

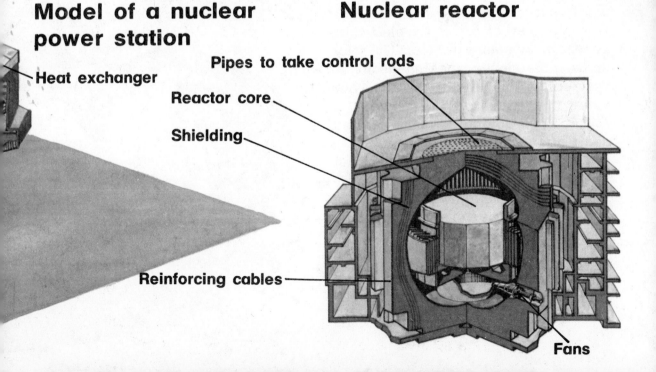

Heat exchanger

Pipes to take control rods

Reactor core

Shielding

Reinforcing cables

Fans

Sun, Wind and Wave Power

The world gets most of its energy by burning coal, oil and natural gas, but these fuels are becoming scarce, and one day they will run out. Then we shall have to use other forms of energy. We shall use, for example, the energy in nature. There is energy in flowing water, wind, sunlight and waves.

We can tap the energy in flowing water with water turbines, to make electricity (see page 48). We can tap the energy in the wind with modern kinds of windmills called wind turbines. One kind of wind turbine is shown here. It has blades like an airplane propeller, which spin in the wind.

The "propeller" part of the turbine is called the rotor. It is mounted on a shaft that goes to a gearbox. A shaft from the gearbox drives the electricity generator by means of belts. The rotor spins quite slowly, making about 40 revolutions per minute (rpm). Then gears in the gearbox increase this to about 1,800 rpm to turn the output shaft and generator.

The wind can be used, then, for making electricity for your home. Sunlight can be used for heating your hot water. To trap the sun's energy you use solar panels. A solar panel is made of metal and is rather like a central heating radiator. It has pipes running through it which carry water. Above the panel there is a glass sheet.

When the sun shines, the panel becomes warm and heats up the water passing through it. The glass panel on top helps trap the sun's heat like a greenhouse does. The hot water is pumped from the panel through the heat exchanger. There it gives up its heat to water going to the house hot-water system.

There are also plans afoot to use wave power, but not in a wading pool! The plan shown uses a floating raft made up of large numbers of vanes

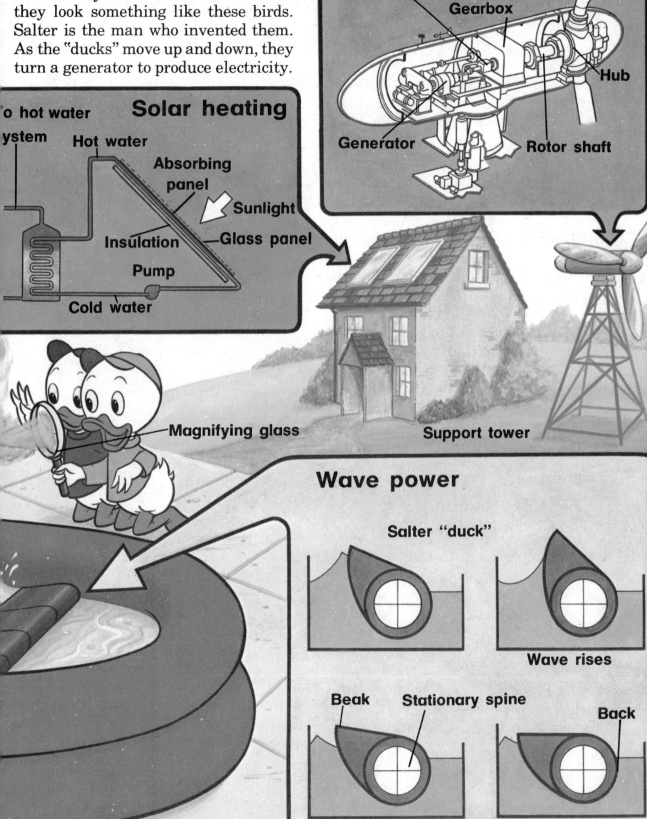

which move up and down with the waves. They are called "ducks" because they look something like these birds. Salter is the man who invented them. As the "ducks" move up and down, they turn a generator to produce electricity.

Wind turbine

Rotor blades

Output shaft

Gearbox

Hub

Generator

Rotor shaft

Solar heating

o hot water ystem

Hot water

Absorbing panel

Sunlight

Insulation

Glass panel

Pump

Cold water

Magnifying glass

Support tower

Wave power

Salter "duck"

Wave rises

Beak   Stationary spine

Back

Wave drops

Farming the Forests

Trees are the biggest and longest-lived plants on Earth. The giant American sequoias, or redwoods, can grow up to 330 feet (100 meters) tall, and the bristle-cone pine can live for up to 5,000 years. Trees provide shelter and homes for a multitude of wildlife, and they provide us with timber.

We use timber not only in building and for making furniture, but also as a raw material to make other products, including paper and artificial fibers. Millions upon millions of trees are felled every year in the world's forests to provide us with timber.

Felling the Trees

Most of the world's timber comes from the great forests of softwoods, which thrive in the cool regions of northern Europe and North America.

The first stage in timber production is felling, or cutting down the trees. In the past tree fellers used hand axes and two-man saws to cut down the trees. Now, however, they use chain saws.

The chain saw has a saw blade which consists of an endless chain with saw teeth attached. The chain is driven around an oval guide bar by a tiny gasoline engine.

The engine has a single cylinder and piston, which drives around a crankshaft by means of a connecting rod. The crankshaft drives the saw chain through a clutch. The clutch consists of inner shoes attached by springs to the crankshaft and an outer drum connected to the chain. When the engine is turning slowly, the springs hold the shoes to the crankshaft. When it is turning quickly, the shoes are flung

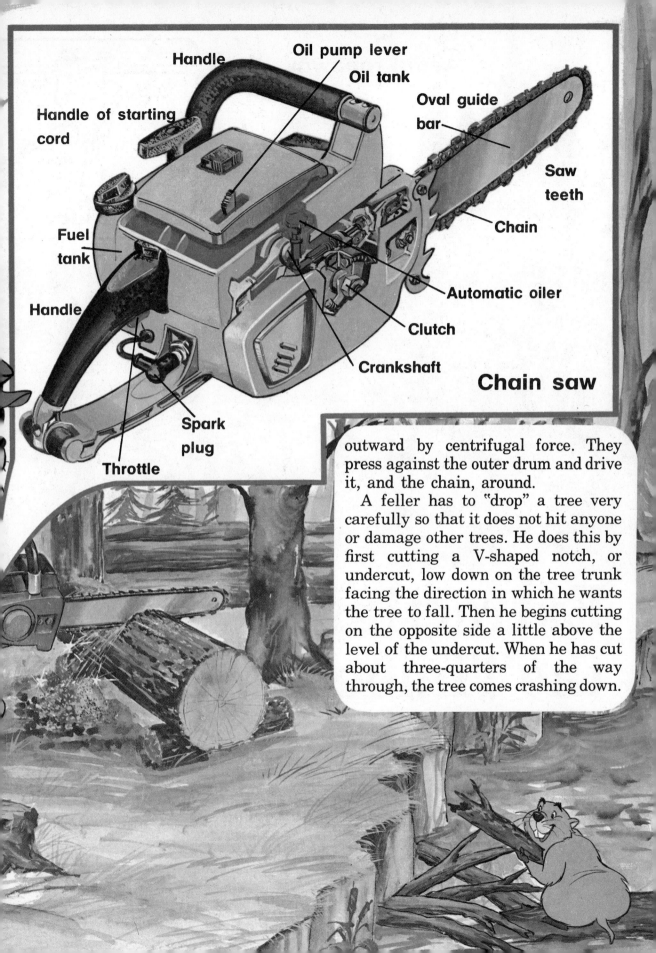

Handle

Oil pump lever

Oil tank

Handle of starting cord

Oval guide bar

Saw teeth

Fuel tank

Chain

Handle

Automatic oiler

Clutch

Crankshaft

Chain saw

Spark plug

Throttle

outward by centrifugal force. They press against the outer drum and drive it, and the chain, around.

A feller has to "drop" a tree very carefully so that it does not hit anyone or damage other trees. He does this by first cutting a V-shaped notch, or undercut, low down on the tree trunk facing the direction in which he wants the tree to fall. Then he begins cutting on the opposite side a little above the level of the undercut. When he has cut about three-quarters of the way through, the tree comes crashing down.

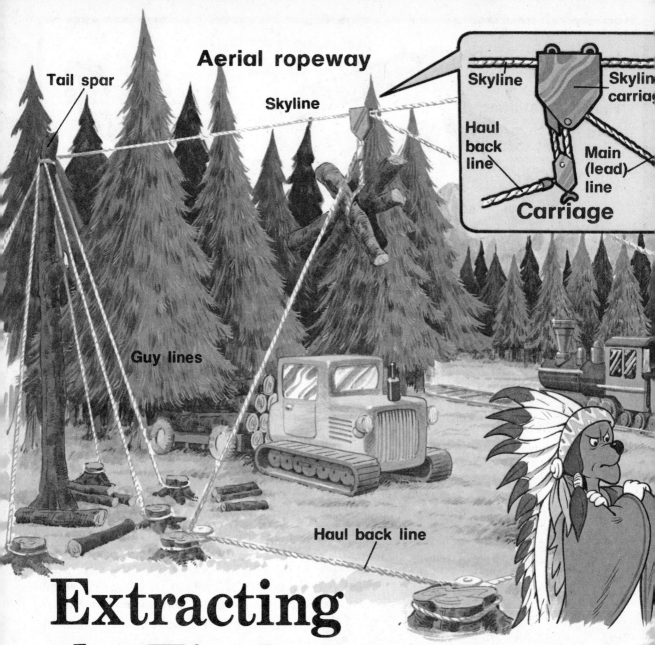

Aerial ropeway

Tail spar

Skyline

Skyline

Skyline carriage

Haul back line

Main (lead) line

Carriage

Guy lines

Haul back line

Extracting the Timber

As soon as the felled tree has hit the ground, another man moves in with a chain saw to lop off the branches and cut the trunk into shorter lengths. The cut timber then has to be removed from the forest either to the sawmill, where it will be cut up into boards; or to the pulpmill, where it will be turned into woodpulp for making paper.

Before the timber is transported from the forest, it is collected at a central point for convenience. This operation is known as extraction. There are several methods of extraction. Caterpillar tractors are often used to haul in the logs. They may simply drag the logs along the ground, or use wheeled frames called arches or sulkies. These frames lift the front end of the logs off the ground, making them easier to haul.

60

Pulley

Head spar

Donkey engine

Another method of extraction widely used is the aerial ropeway, which can carry logs over great distances. The picture shows a simple one in use. In an aerial system, a few of the tallest trees in the forest are left standing and used as "spar trees." Then cables are slung between them and pulled taut. They form a path along which a carriage can travel carrying the logs. Lines (cables) attached to the carriage pull it back and forth. They are hauled by a power winch, via a system of pulleys.

A simpler system uses a single spar tree with a pulley on top. A cable goes from a winch up and over the pulley, and its end is attached to the logs. The winch then hauls in the cable, dragging in the logs as it does so.

The logs may be transported in various ways from the forest. In some regions it may be possible to transport them by road or rail. If no road or railway exists, then temporary ones may have to be built.

Floating the Logs

In many of the huge timber forests of the north there are no convenient roads or railways for transporting the felled timber, but there are rivers and lakes. These provide a convenient means of transportation because timber floats.

When the rivers freeze in the winter, the logs are piled up on the bank. When the thaw arrives, the logs are rolled into the swift-flowing water. When they jam together, as they often do, a team of log "drivers" armed with long spiked poles is on hand to break them up and keep them moving. The drivers often have to climb on to the logs to reach the jams, which is a very dangerous thing to do.

On wide rivers and across lakes, the logs may be bound together to form rafts and then towed by tugs. Alternatively, they may be enclosed in a huge floating boom, which is then towed.

Eventually, either by water, truck or train, the logs arrive at the sawmill. There they are often stored, not on dry land but in a vast log pond. They are stored in water for several reasons. There is less risk of fire and of attack by insects and fungi, which could damage the wood. While the logs are stored, workmen examine and grade them.

The logs are fed one by one into the mill through a chute by a chain conveyor. Just before the logs enter the mill they are sprayed by powerful jets of water. This treatment removes any dirt and stones that might have become trapped in the bark. Such materials could easily damage the saws.

Log boom

Tug

Spiked pole

Log conveyor

U-shaped trough

Endless chain

Log

Water level

Log pond

In the Sawmill

In the sawmill the logs are cut into timber of the shapes and sizes needed by timber merchants. As a log enters the mill, it is clamped on to a carriage and then fed against the saw that slices it into board. Sometimes the outer bark is first removed by a circular saw.

The first main saw in the mill may be a frame saw or a band saw. The frame saw consists of a number of saw blades set in a frame. The frame moves rapidly up and down to give a sawing action. A frame saw can convert a complete log into boards in one operation, but it is not suitable for sawing logs of very large diameter.

The other main kind of saw is the vertical band saw. This consists of an endless steel band with saw teeth cut in it. It travels around two large wheels, one of which drives it at high speed. The carriage holding the log moves back and forth, feeding the log against the saw every time it moves forward. The log is thus converted into board, slice by slice.

Other sets of saws in the sawmill are used to cut the boards into the shapes, lengths and thicknesses required and trim them square.

The sawn timber is not yet ready for use because it is "green," or contains too much moisture. It needs to be carefully dried, otherwise it could warp (twist and bend) and split. Timber is often dried, or seasoned, in the air. It is simply stacked in open racks under covers to keep off the rain. Air season-

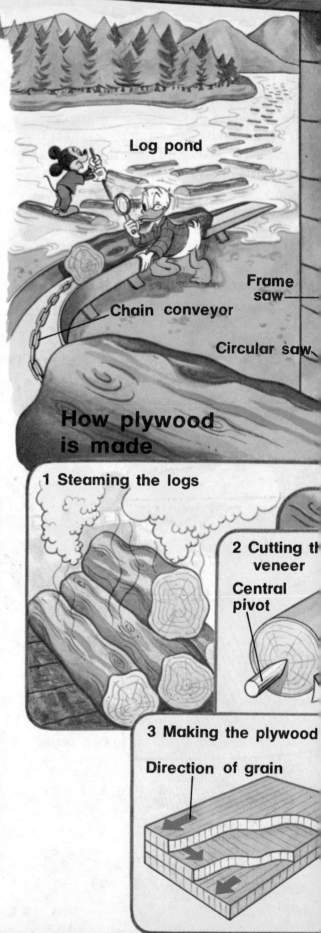

Log pond

Frame saw

Chain conveyor

Circular saw

How plywood is made

1 Steaming the logs

2 Cutting the veneer

Central pivot

3 Making the plywood

Direction of grain

ing can take up to a year or even longer, and that is why timber is now often seasoned in a special oven, or kiln. Kiln seasoning is much quicker, often taking only a few weeks.

In some mills the logs are converted into thin sheets of wood, or veneer, and made into plywood. The logs are rotated against a sharp knife blade, and the veneer peels off in a continuous ribbon. Plywood is made by glueing sheets of veneer together in a special way. They are glued so that the grain, or direction of the wood fibers, in one sheet is at right-angles to the grain in the sheets on either side. This makes plywood much stronger than natural wood of the same thickness.

Timber being seasoned

Slices of veneer

Cutting blade

Moving carriage

Fighting Forest Fires

Lookout tower

Firefighters

Firefighting plane

Fire tender

The trees in the forest are attacked by insects and fungi and may be chewed by animals such as rabbits and deer, but their biggest enemy by far is fire. Most of the world's great timber forests are conifers, such as pine trees, and the trunks of these trees contain much resin, which burns readily. In a dry summer even a spark can set the forest ablaze. With the wind behind it, a forest fire can travel faster than a man can run. In most forests there are wide breaks in the trees, at regular intervals. These are not only used as roads, but act as firebreaks to help prevent a fire spreading, should it break out.

Foresters keep a constant watch for fire from tall lookout towers among the treetops. They have maps and instruments which help them locate the exact position of any fire they see flare up in the forest. They can then direct the firefighters to the scene without any delay.

If there are streams near the fire, then water can be used to help put it out. If there are no streams, then water may be dropped from the air from converted cargo planes. In out-of-the-way places, even the firefighters may have to be dropped from the air by parachute.

When a forest fire gets really under way, it cannot be stopped by ordinary means. One method of fighting it is to make a fire line well in advance of the fire. This is done by clearing a broad belt of all vegetation, to act as a barrier to the flame. The trees on the side toward the fire can also be deliberately fired so that it burns toward the main fire. Then, it is hoped, the two fires will meet and burn themselves out, but this does not always work.

Mining

A great many of the materials we use in our everyday lives came originally from the ground. Our metals, for example, are found locked in the minerals of the rocks. Our important fuel coal is also found trapped in the rock layers. We also need large amounts of stone and gravel for building purposes. The mining industry has developed to take

and Quarrying

out, or extract, minerals and coal from the ground.

Man has been a miner for thousands of years. At first he simply dug out the materials he wanted where he found them on the surface. Then he began tunneling underground to reach deposits.

Quarrying

Concrete is one of our main building materials. We use it to build homes, skyscrapers, bridges, dams and roads.

The chalk, clay, sand, gravel and stone chips needed to make concrete are extracted from great open pits in the ground known as quarries. Vast quantities of other useful materials are also taken from the ground. For example, limestone rock is quarried for use in industry.

Removing sand and gravel from the ground is easy. They are soft deposits which can simply be removed by power shovels and excavators. Harder rock

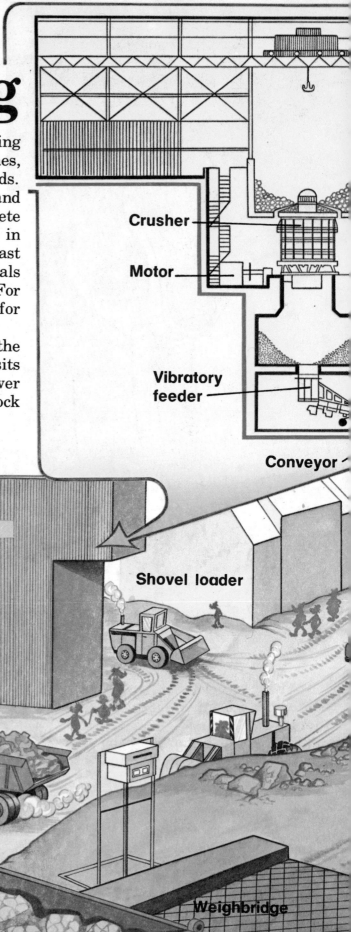

Crusher

Motor

Vibratory feeder

Conveyor

Primary crusher

Shovel loader

Dumper trucks

Truck being weighed

Weighbridge

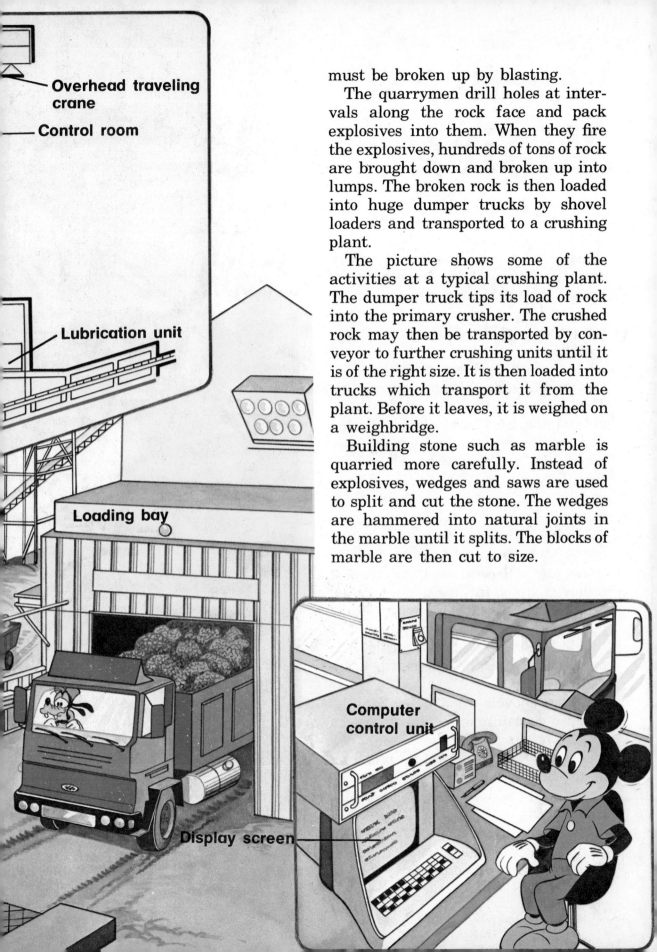

Overhead traveling crane

Control room

Lubrication unit

Loading bay

Computer control unit

Display screen

must be broken up by blasting.

The quarrymen drill holes at intervals along the rock face and pack explosives into them. When they fire the explosives, hundreds of tons of rock are brought down and broken up into lumps. The broken rock is then loaded into huge dumper trucks by shovel loaders and transported to a crushing plant.

The picture shows some of the activities at a typical crushing plant. The dumper truck tips its load of rock into the primary crusher. The crushed rock may then be transported by conveyor to further crushing units until it is of the right size. It is then loaded into trucks which transport it from the plant. Before it leaves, it is weighed on a weighbridge.

Building stone such as marble is quarried more carefully. Instead of explosives, wedges and saws are used to split and cut the stone. The wedges are hammered into natural joints in the marble until it splits. The blocks of marble are then cut to size.

Opencast Mining

As well as rock and gravel, we take vast quantities of other materials from the ground to use in industry. These are deposits of coal and numerous minerals. The most important class of minerals are those we call ores. Ores are minerals that can be processed into metals.

We call the process of taking coal and minerals from the ground, mining. The deposits often lie deep underground and must be reached by boring and tunneling into the ground (see pages 76-79). Sometimes, however, they lie on or near the surface of the ground and mining is then much easier.

Mining from the surface is called opencast mining. In the mining operations, any soil covering the deposit is removed by giant excavators called draglines. They excavate with a huge bucket, which they cast outward rather like a fisherman casts his tackle. The bucket scoops up the soil as it is dragged back.

Power shovels then scoop up the exposed deposit and load it into trucks for transport from the mine. The trucks may take it first to a crushing plant to be reduced to a suitable size. Sometimes the deposit is removed continuously by excavators that scoop it up with rotating buckets. The buckets feed the deposit on to conveyor belts that remove it for loading into trucks.

Coal Mining

Coal is not an ordinary mineral, like iron ore, for example. Minerals are the chemical substances that make up the rocks of the Earth. Coal is mainly carbon. It is the remains of things that once lived; of plants that grew in the swamps that covered much of the Earth several hundred million years ago. They were plants similar to the ferns and horsetails found today, but hundreds of times bigger, as big as our tallest trees today.

After these giant plants died, they fell into the swamp and were buried under more plant material, mud and clay. Gradually they began to rot, and the pressure of the material above them squeezed out the water they contained.

In time, measured in many millions of years, the clay and mud layers turned into hard rock and the plant material turned into coal.

In some parts of the world the coal layers, or seams, are found close to the surface. Then they can be mined by opencast methods (page 72). Often, however, the coal seams lie deep underground, sandwiched between the rocks.

At an underground coal mine, or pit, vertical shafts are bored into the ground and then horizontal tunnels are driven outward from them to the coal seams.

The miners travel up and down the pit shafts in elevators, or cages. Elevators also carry the wagon loads of coal to the surface. The winding gear which moves the elevators consists of large wheels on top of a triangular tower. The cables that support the elevators go up and over the wheels, which are driven by a powerful engine in the winding house.

There are several other buildings at the pithead. In one the coal lifted from

Miner

Coal wagon

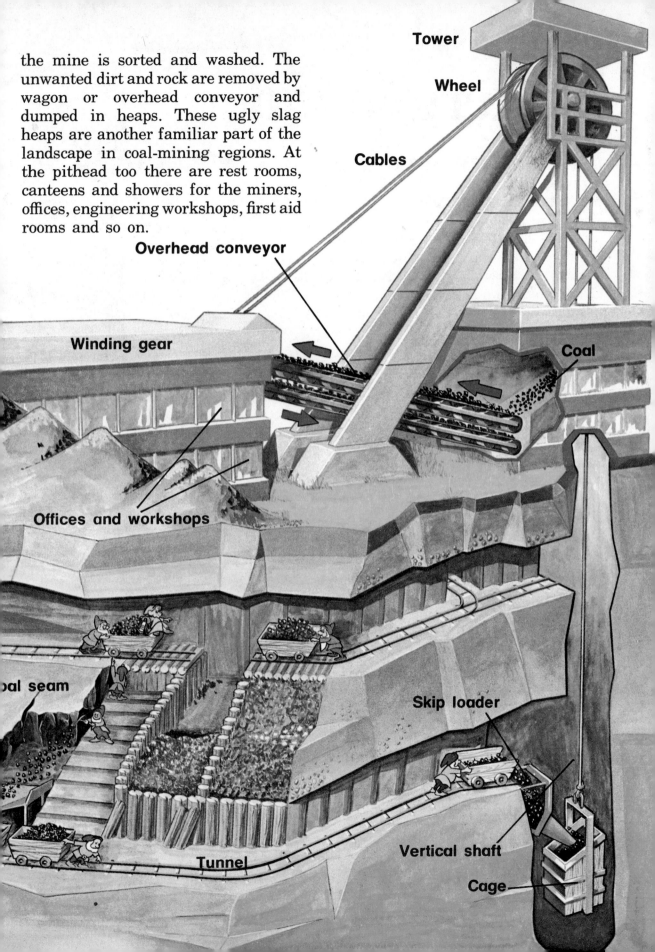

the mine is sorted and washed. The unwanted dirt and rock are removed by wagon or overhead conveyor and dumped in heaps. These ugly slag heaps are another familiar part of the landscape in coal-mining regions. At the pithead too there are rest rooms, canteens and showers for the miners, offices, engineering workshops, first aid rooms and so on.

Tower

Wheel

Cables

Overhead conveyor

Winding gear

Coal

Offices and workshops

Coal seam

Skip loader

Tunnel

Vertical shaft

Cage

Underground

In a large coal mine the underground tunnels lead for many miles in different directions at different levels. There are not only shafts to carry the miners and coal wagons, but also ventilation shafts through which air is sucked or blown by powerful fans. Good ventilation is essential in mines because of the dusty atmosphere. It also helps prevent the build-up of dangerous gases, which could suffocate the miners or cause an explosion.

If the coal face on which they are working is far from the pit shaft, the miners travel to it by railway. They ride in simple low cars pulled by a small diesel or battery-powered locomotive. Locomotives also haul the wagon loads of coal from the coal face. Until quite recently ponies were mainly used to haul the wagons. In some old mines pit ponies are still used today. Trough conveyors are now also widely used to move the coal underground.

The main underground tunnels are lined with concrete and steel ribs, or arches, which prevent the roof caving in. In the side tunnels and galleries

Winding house

Rock strata

Abandoned seam

Coal seam

Elevator (cage)

Coal shearer

Elevator sh

Conveyor/loader

Coal seam

Main tunnel

Railway

Auxiliary dynamo/pump

Pumping house

Ventilation shaft

Rock strata

Coal seam

Gallery

Gallery

Coal wagon

Miner's lamp

Rock fault

Locomotive

close to the coal face temporary roof supports are provided by pit props. These may be removed after the coal has been extracted.

The coal itself may be removed, or "won," with the help of explosives, as in mineral mining. First the miners use a coalcutter to make an undercut in the coal face. The coalcutter is rather like a big chainsaw (page 58). It cuts with an endless cutting chain, which revolves around a flat blade.

After undercutting, the miners drill holes in the coal face, insert explosive charges, and fire them. The blast brings down part of the coal face, which is then loaded into wagons or on to conveyors for transport to the pit-shaft.

In many modern mines, however, the miners use machines to mine the coal without explosives (page 78). These machines can only be used when the coal seams are thick and level.

Machine Mining

Coal is very different from the other kinds of minerals miners dig from the ground. It is the remains of things that were once living – giant ferns which lived in swampy forests many millions of years ago. Also, coal is quite soft – soft enough to cut with machinery, and in many mines these days, machines are used to help dig out the coal.

Some miners use a coalcutter, which is a bigger version of the power chainsaw lumberjacks use to fell trees. Miners use it to make an undercut at the bottom of the coal face. Then they drill holes into the coal face and fill them with explosive. When the explosive fires, the face is broken up and falls down. Power loaders then shovel the coal into wagons, or on to conveyor belts, which haul it to the elevator shaft.

In many mines now, throughout the world, the whole coalcutting, loading and conveying process is automatic. The main machine used is called a shearer. It moves back and forth along the coal face, cutting the coal continuously as it does so. It has one or more cutting heads, which are large rotating drums studded with cutting teeth.

As the cutting head revolves, it bites into the coal seam and breaks off the coal in lumps. The lumps fall on to an endless chain or plate conveyor, which removes it. The shearer is driven by hydraulic (liquid pressure) motors along a track. While it works, it is protected from damage by falling rocks by hydraulic pit props. These are often called "walking props" because they move forward step by step and one by one as the coalface is cut away.

Whatever method of coal mining is used underground, it is dirty, dusty work, and there is also a danger of explosions from an inflammable gas known as firedamp. Its proper name is methane, which is also the main gas in the mixture of gases we use for heating and cooking in the home. In the early days miners used candles for lighting in mines, which was very dangerous. Then Sir Humphry Davy in 1815

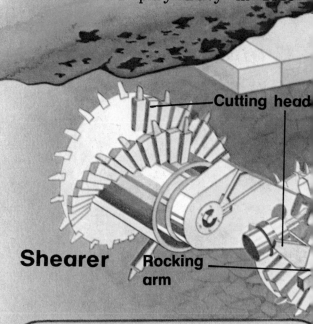

Shearer — Cutting head — Rocking arm

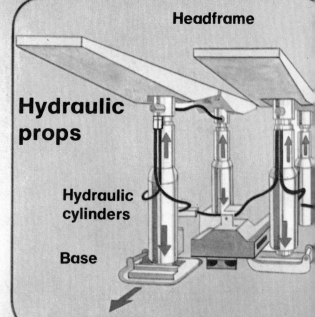

Hydraulic props — Headframe — Hydraulic cylinders — Base

invented a safety oil lamp, which didn't set off firedamp. The Davy lamp has its flame enclosed by a gauze, which conducts the heat of the flame away and stops the firedamp exploding.

These days miners use battery-operated helmet lamps, but they still often use the safety lamp to detect firedamp. The size of the flame changes when firedamp is present.

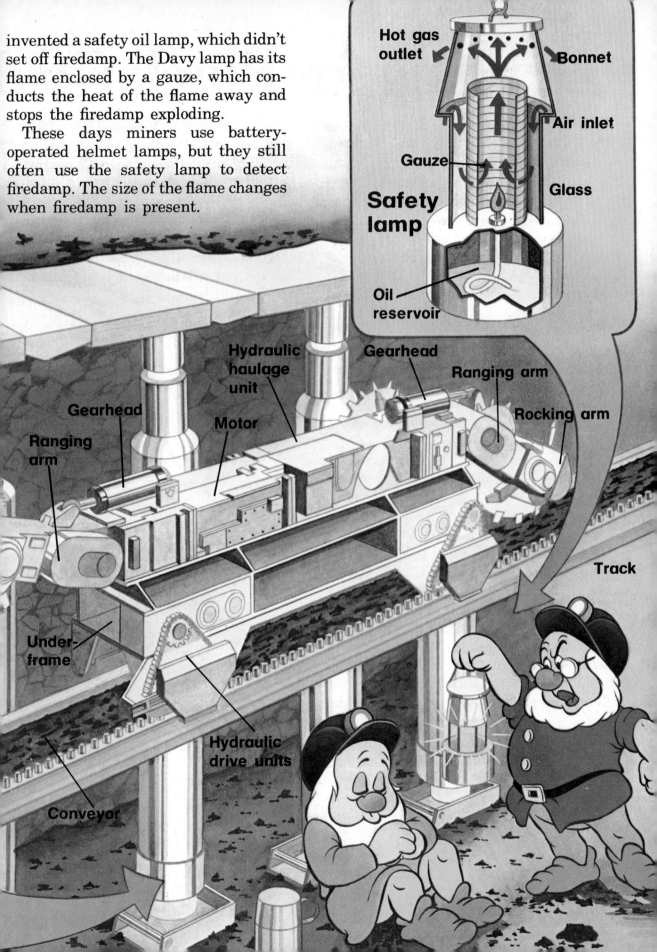

Hot gas outlet

Bonnet

Air inlet

Gauze

Glass

Safety lamp

Oil reservoir

Hydraulic haulage unit

Gearhead

Ranging arm

Rocking arm

Gearhead

Motor

Ranging arm

Track

Under-frame

Hydraulic drive units

Conveyor

Drilling for Black Gold

The most important of the fuels we use today is oil, which we get by drilling deep down into the rocks. Oil is the remains of minute creatures and plants that lived in ancient seas. When they died, their remains slowly changed into drops of oil. Over millions of years the oil moved through the pores, or holes, in the rocks until it came up against rock so solid that it became trapped. It is into such traps that we drill for oil.

Oil is often called "black gold" because it is so precious. It provides us not only with fuels like gasoline and kerosene, but also with other chemicals. As it is taken from the ground, oil is a thick greenish-black substance known as "crude." Crude oil has to be processed in an oil refinery before it is useful.

Drilling for crude oil is carried out on land and at sea. Drilling at sea is more difficult. The equipment used for drilling is dominated by a tall steel tower, or derrick. The derrick and other equipment form an oil rig.

Drilling is done with a rotating drill, which bores through rock. The drill consists of a long pipe at the bottom of which is a cutting bit. The pipe is made up of many lengths of tubing screwed

together. As the borehole deepens, extra lengths of tubing are added. At the top of the drill pipe is a tube called the kelly, which has four or six sides. This is gripped in a turntable and rotated to carry out the drilling. As drilling proceeds, the borehole is usually lined with a steel casing.

When extra lengths of tubing must

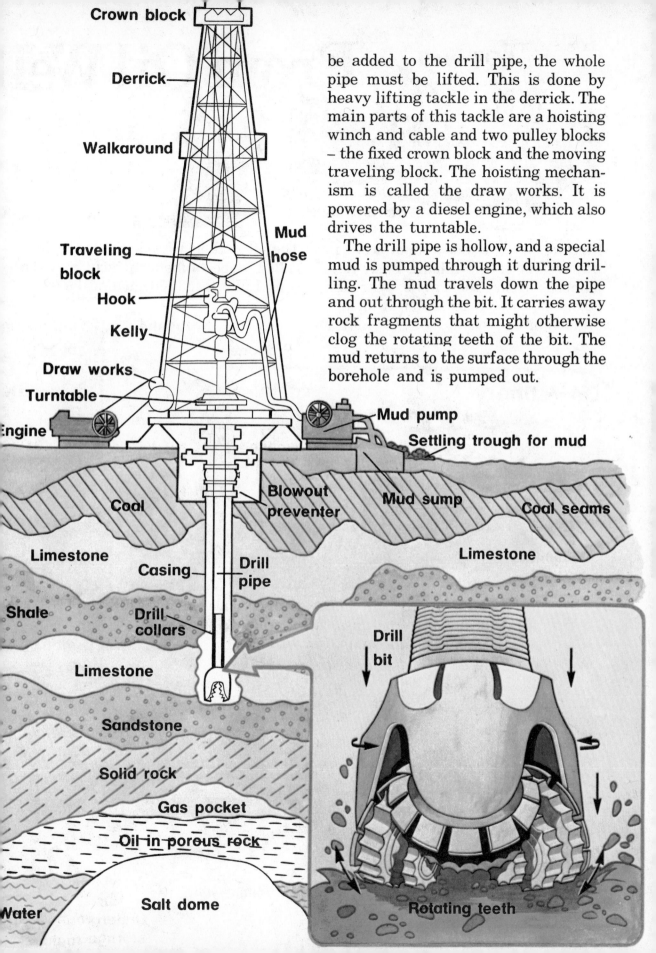

Crown block

Derrick

Walkaround

Traveling block

Hook

Kelly

Draw works

Turntable

Engine

Mud hose

Mud pump

Settling trough for mud

Mud sump

Blowout preventer

Coal

Coal seams

Limestone

Limestone

Casing

Drill pipe

Shale

Drill collars

Limestone

Sandstone

Solid rock

Gas pocket

Oil in porous rock

Water

Salt dome

Drill bit

Rotating teeth

be added to the drill pipe, the whole pipe must be lifted. This is done by heavy lifting tackle in the derrick. The main parts of this tackle are a hoisting winch and cable and two pulley blocks – the fixed crown block and the moving traveling block. The hoisting mechanism is called the draw works. It is powered by a diesel engine, which also drives the turntable.

The drill pipe is hollow, and a special mud is pumped through it during drilling. The mud travels down the pipe and out through the bit. It carries away rock fragments that might otherwise clog the rotating teeth of the bit. The mud returns to the surface through the borehole and is pumped out.

Oil well

From Oil Well

Storage tank

Much of our oil comes from oil wells in the deserts of the Middle East. It is pumped from the wells, through pipelines, to storage tanks at oil terminals on the coast.

The oil is then loaded into huge ships called supertankers, which may be over 1,300 feet (400 meters) long.

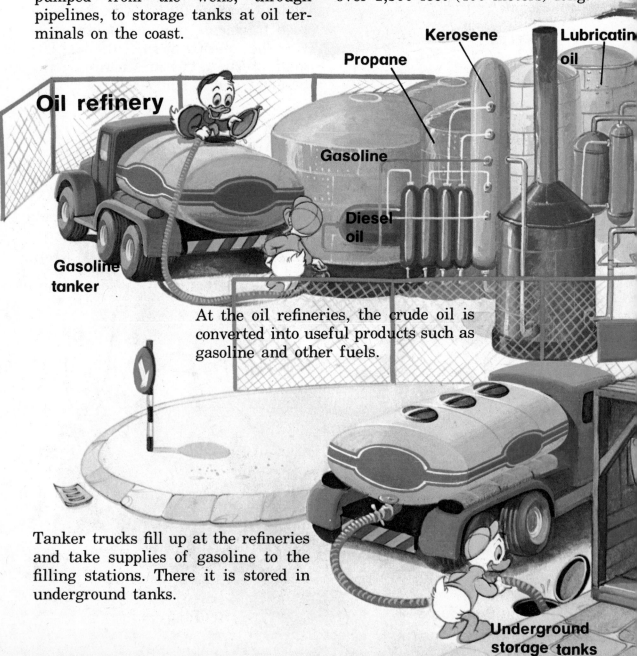

Oil refinery

Propane

Kerosene

Lubricating oil

Gasoline

Diesel oil

Gasoline tanker

At the oil refineries, the crude oil is converted into useful products such as gasoline and other fuels.

Tanker trucks fill up at the refineries and take supplies of gasoline to the filling stations. There it is stored in underground tanks.

Underground storage tanks

to Fuel Tank

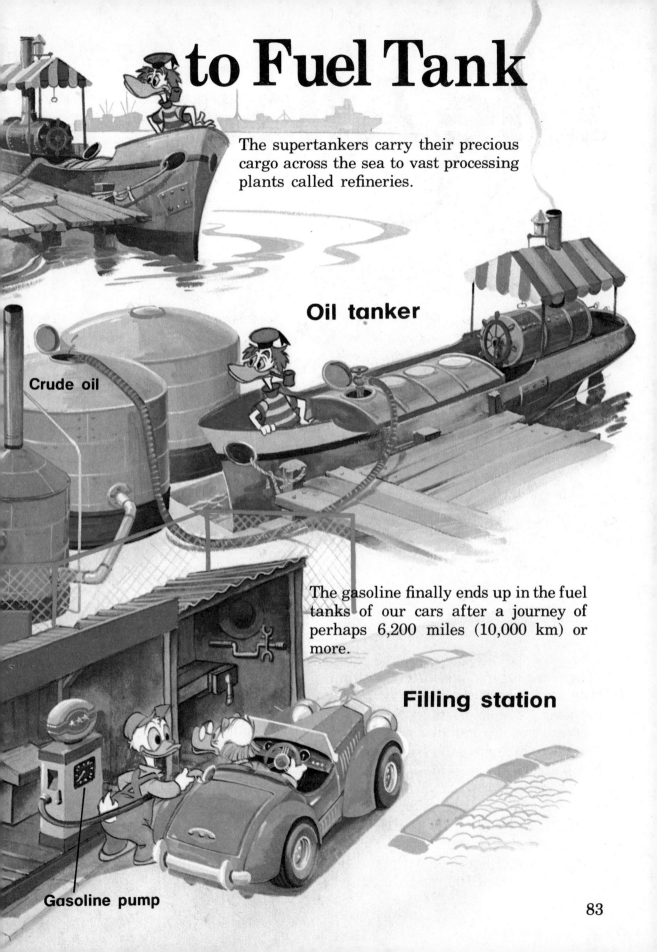

The supertankers carry their precious cargo across the sea to vast processing plants called refineries.

Oil tanker

Crude oil

The gasoline finally ends up in the fuel tanks of our cars after a journey of perhaps 6,200 miles (10,000 km) or more.

Filling station

Gasoline pump

Life Afloat

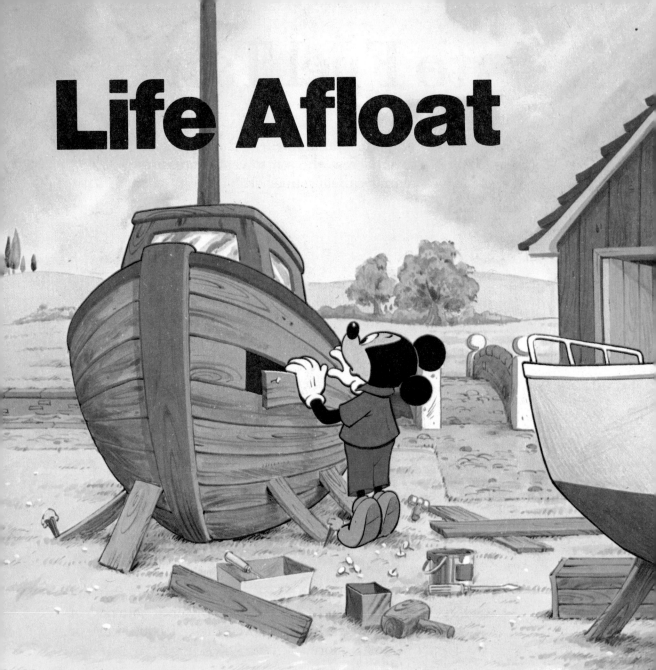

"There is nothing, absolutely nothing, half so much worth doing as simply messing about in boats."

Most of us would agree with Ratty's remark to his newfound friend Moly in Kenneth Grahame's delightful children's book *The Wind in the Willows*. Messing about in boats is great fun – it is even fascinating to watch other people messing about!

It has something to do with the ever-changing mood of the water, its differ-rent smells and noises, and the feeling of being close to nature. On boats, whatever kind they are, there is always something to be done. There are sails to be set, charts to be checked, sandbanks to be avoided, locks to be negotiated, tides to be caught, moorings to be found and anchors to be weighed.

Setting Sail

Many of us begin boating in a small rowboat. You propel yourself with a pair of oars, which pivot in U-shaped rowlocks (pronounced rollocks). You actually travel backward when rowing, with your back toward the bow (front of the boat) and your face toward the stern (rear).

Rowing is always tiring, especially if the wind and the current are against you. For reasonably long trips it is wise to have an outboard motor also. This is a self-contained unit made up of a small engine and a coupled propeller. It is mounted at the stern and can usually pivot on its mounting so that the propeller comes out of the water. This is necessary when you want to beach the boat.

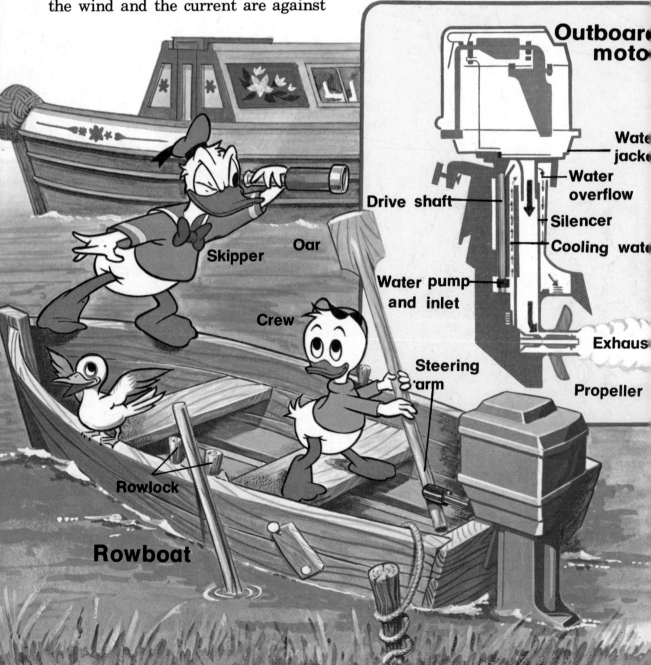

Outboard motor

Water jacket

Water overflow

Silencer

Cooling water

Drive shaft

Water pump and inlet

Steering arm

Exhaust

Propeller

Skipper

Oar

Crew

Rowlock

Rowboat

Sailboat

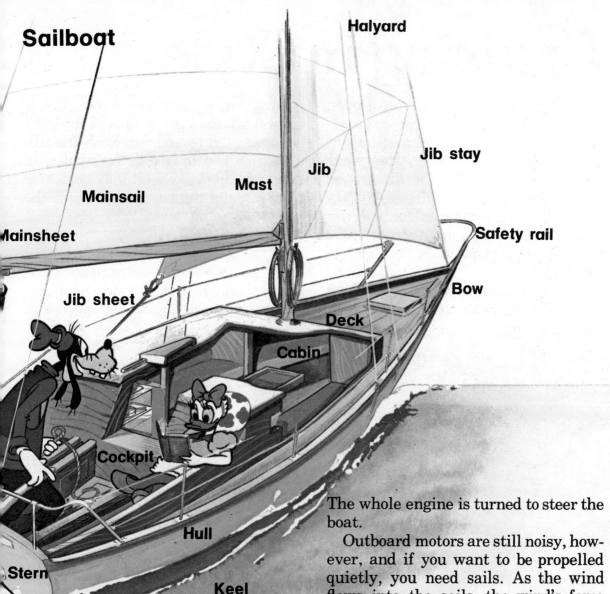

Halyard

Jib stay

Jib

Mast

Mainsail

Safety rail

Mainsheet

Bow

Jib sheet

Deck

Cabin

Cockpit

Hull

Stern

Keel

Rudder

The outboard motor has a gasoline engine which is often started with a pull cord, like many lawn mowers. The engine drives a shaft that extends vertically downward to a short shaft (propshaft) that carries the propeller. The engine is cooled by water being pumped through it. In modern designs a water jacket surrounds the engine exhaust pipe, which discharges under water. This helps silence the engine.

The whole engine is turned to steer the boat.

Outboard motors are still noisy, however, and if you want to be propelled quietly, you need sails. As the wind flows into the sails, the wind's force pushes the boat along. To change direction you need to manipulate and turn the sails to catch the wind just right. The wind's force can also push you sideways. This is why a sailboat is built with a keel under its hull. The keel helps prevent the boat being pushed sideways.

There are many kinds of sailboats. The one illustrated is a simple sloop with a single mast and two triangular sails. Others have different rigs, or mast-and-sail arrangements.

Cruising in Style

The simplest sailing craft have open decks with simple seating arrangements. Others have enclosed cabins and many home comforts. They have much the same kind of fittings as trailers. In addition to the sails, they may have engines fitted for use, for example, when the weather is calm, when maneuvering in a harbor, or when mooring.

A typical family yacht has a saloon containing four berths (beds), which

pulling in or letting go the sheets (ropes) attached to the sails as the wind changes, and by steering with the tiller, which is attached to the rudder. In larger boats the cockpit may be nearer the center of the boat, from which the rudder is controlled remotely by a wheel.

In the cockpit of the boat there will also be several instruments and gauges, which give the skipper information about his engine and speed, and

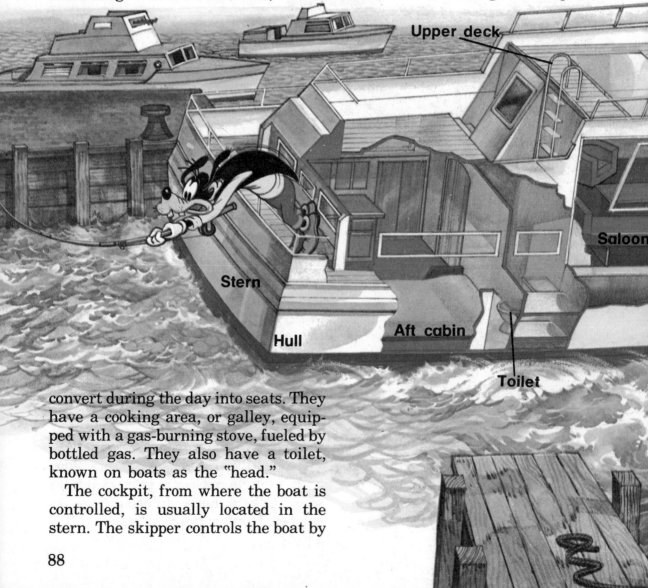

convert during the day into seats. They have a cooking area, or galley, equipped with a gas-burning stove, fueled by bottled gas. They also have a toilet, known on boats as the "head."

The cockpit, from where the boat is controlled, is usually located in the stern. The skipper controls the boat by

help him navigate. The two most vital navigation instruments are the compass and echo sounder. The compass shows the skipper what course he is on while the echo sounder tells him what depth of water is beneath the hull.

Ocean-going cabin cruisers like the one shown in the picture have all the features of the family motor-sailing craft, and many more besides. It has many more berths in separate cabins, an enclosed wheelhouse instead of an open cockpit, and several decks.

Among additional equipment, it would probably have a two-way radio or radio-telephone and radar.

Most family yachts and cabin cruisers are now being built of fiberglass, or glass-reinforced plastic (GRP) as it is properly called. GRP is tough and completely waterproof and needs much less maintenance than the traditional wooden-hulled vessels. The boat hulls are made by building up layers of plastic and fiberglass matting around a shaped mold.

Cabin cruiser

Wheelhouse

Shower room

Dinette

Bow

Galley

(forward cabin)

Double sink unit

Stove

Inflatable dinghy

Outboard motor

89

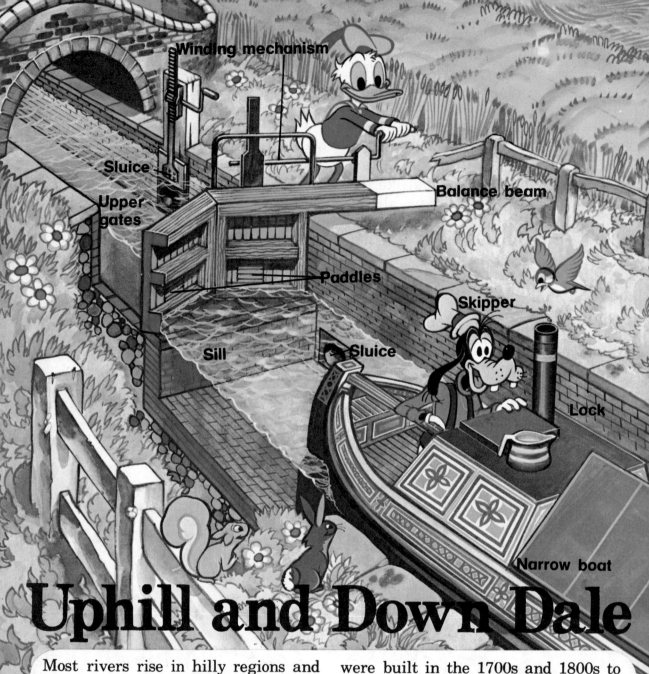

Winding mechanism

Sluice

Upper gates

Balance beam

Paddles

Skipper

Sill

Sluice

Lock

Narrow boat

Uphill and Down Dale

Most rivers rise in hilly regions and flow gradually downhill until they run into the sea or a lake, but you only really notice that they change levels at waterfalls or dams. If you are traveling by boat, you need a way to go from one level to another. Locks are for this purpose. They raise boats up or lower them, whichever is necessary.

There are usually more locks, however, on canals than on rivers. Canals are artificial waterways. Most canals

were built in the 1700s and 1800s to provide better transportation of coal and other materials between the mines and the industries to the factories that use them.

Most of the canals were built quite narrow, and special boats were built for them, called narrow boats. At first the narrow boats were pulled by horses, who plodded along a towpath at the side of the canal. Later boats had steam engines. Today only a few canals are still in use, and the craft which sail them are pleasure boats.

The picture shows a narrow boat in a canal lock going from a higher (left) to a lower level. There are heavy wooden gates at each end. They form a V-shape with the bottom of the V pointing upstream. With this arrangement the pressure of the water tends to keep them closed.

You operate the lock by letting water flow into and out of it through sluices and paddles in the gates. You can open the gates only when the water level on each side is the same.

The diagram shows how a typical lock works, though the sluice arrangement may differ slightly from lock to lock. A boat at the lower level is waiting to enter the lock (1). The lower gates open to let it inside (2). The gates are then closed and the inlet sluice is opened (3), allowing water from upstream to flow into the lock and raise the boat to the upper level. The upper gates can then be opened and the boat can then sail out. To empty the lock, the upper sluice and gates are closed, and the paddles in the lower gates are opened (4).

Lock operation

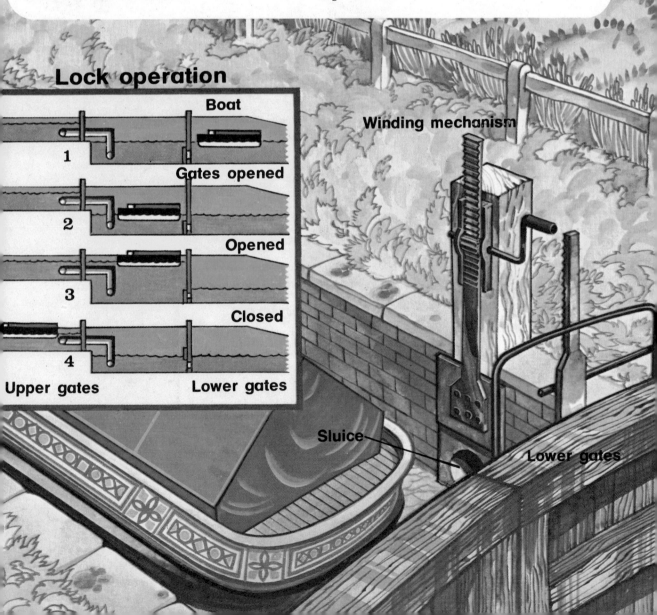

Boat

1

Gates opened

2

Opened

3

Closed

4

Upper gates   **Lower gates**

Winding mechanism

Sluice

Lower gates

Paddle Power

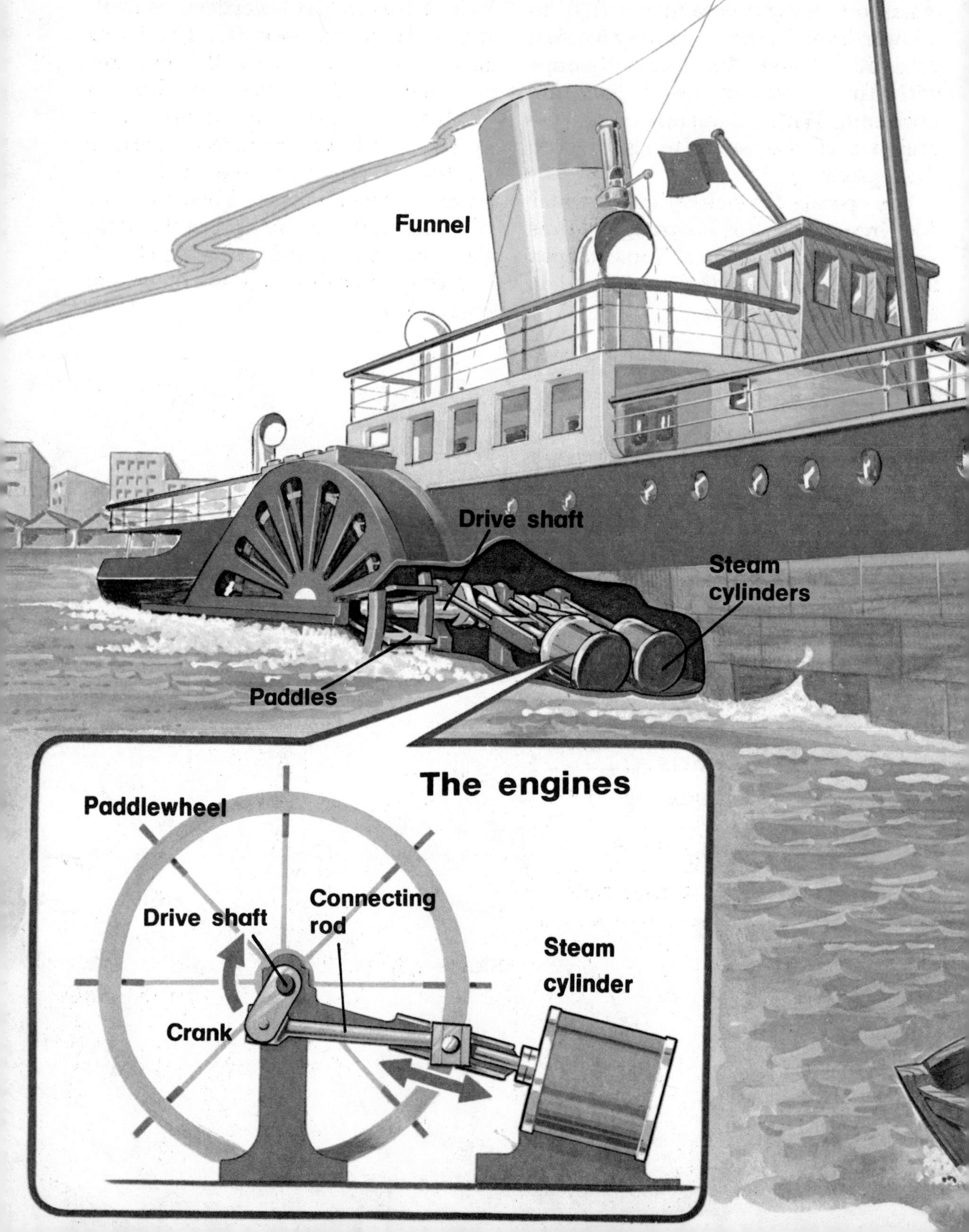

Funnel

Drive shaft

Steam cylinders

Paddles

The engines

Paddlewheel

Drive shaft

Connecting rod

Steam cylinder

Crank

Practically all powered boats these days are propelled by a propeller spinning beneath the water. The propeller is so shaped that it "screws" itself through the water – it is often called a "screw," and is located at the stern.

A few pleasure craft have a different method of propulsion – the paddle wheel. A paddle wheel is either a wheel or a cylinder with wooden slats projecting from the side. The paddles dip into the water as the wheel turns, creating a continuous paddling action that drives the boat.

Usually paddle wheels are powered by steam engines, and boats with them are called paddle steamers. The paddle steamer in the picture has twin paddle wheels mounted at the sides. They are driven by steam piston engines through a connecting rod and crankshaft.

Steam is raised in the paddle steamer's boilers and piped to the steam cylinders. In the cylinders the steam expands and pushes against a piston. A connecting rod connects the piston to a crank on the drive shaft. When the piston moves, the connecting rod turns the crank and thus the drive shaft and paddle wheel. Steam is introduced to each side of the piston in turn.

The first successful power boats built used side paddle wheels to propel them. The earliest was the *Clermont*, built in 1807 by Robert Fulton in the United States. The early steamships also used side paddle wheels until the mid-1800s, when the screw propeller came into use. Paddle steamers still remained popular for much longer on many rivers.

The most famous paddle wheel river craft were the flat-bottomed Mississippi steamboats, such as the *Robert E. Lee*. Paddle steamboats can still be seen on the Mississippi at New Orleans today. They are propelled, not by twin side wheels, but by a single cylindrical wheel at the stern (rear).

Water, Water Everywhere

Water is one of the most common substances on Earth. Nearly three-quarters of the Earth's surface is covered with water – seawater. All living things contain water – our own bodies are two-thirds water, and without water nothing on Earth could live.

In our everyday lives we all use vast quantities of water in one form or another. We use it not only to drink, but also to wash with, to flush the toilets, and so on. Industries also use enormous quantities of water. They use it not only in chemical processes, but also for cooling purposes. A steam turbine power station, for example, uses 50 million gallons (225 million liters) of cooling water every hour!

Well, Well, Well

Water table

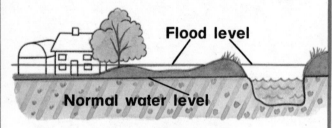

Flood level

Normal water level

Solid rock

Water level in soil is always higher than river level.

Artesian well

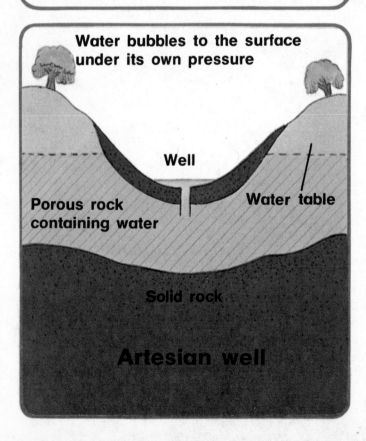

Water bubbles to the surface under its own pressure

Well

Porous rock containing water

Water table

Solid rock

Lift pump

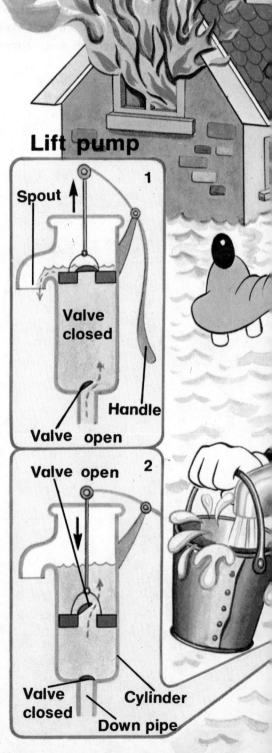

Spout

1

Valve closed

Valve open

Handle

Valve open

2

Valve closed

Cylinder

Down pipe

The water that exists on Earth goes through a never-ending cycle, which we call the water cycle. We can trace the water from the sea and back again. All the time, the water in the sea is evaporating – it is changing into vapor. It evaporates faster as it gets warmer. Water also evaporates from plants as they grow. The water vapor rises into the air, and as it does so it cools and condenses, or changes back into little droplets of water. They form clouds. Eventually the droplets in the clouds get so big that they start to fall as rain (or as snow if the temperature is low enough).

The rain falls on the ground and much of it runs into streams and rivers. The rivers run into lakes or eventually into the sea to complete the cycle. A lot of rainwater also soaks into the soil and flows underground. There it is known as ground water, and the level it reaches at any place is called the water table.

Although most of our water supplies come from lakes, some comes from holes, or wells, sunk into the ground below the water table. In some areas the water may gush to the surface when a well is bored in the ground. Then it is called an artesian well. The natural pressure of the water in the rocks makes this happen (see box).

With most wells, however, you have to pump the water to the surface. The simplest pump is the lift pump shown in the main picture. This can pump water from depths down to about 33 feet (10 meters) beneath the surface. The pump has a piston which is moved up and down inside a cylinder by the handle. A pipe leads from the bottom of the cylinder to the underground water supply. There is a one way valve in the piston and at the top of the down pipe.

When the handle is pumped down (1), the piston valve closes and water is sucked up through the open down pipe valve. When the handle is pumped up (2), the down pipe valve closes and water goes through the piston valve. On the next downstroke of the handle, the water above the piston is lifted up, and pours out of the spout (1).

Purifying the Water

The water that comes from most wells is pure enough to drink. This is because it has passed through many miles of soil since it first fell to the ground as rain (or snow). The soil acts as a filter and removes bits of rotting plant and animal material.

Most of our water, however, comes from surface water in lakes or rivers, and this has to be purified in water treatment plants, or waterworks, before it is fit to drink.

Water supply may be taken from a manmade lake, or reservoir, and piped to the waterworks, or it may be taken from a river and stored in a local reservoir before being piped to the waterworks. After use, the water is piped to a sewage treatment plant.

When the water from the reservoir enters the waterworks, it goes through a number of processes which purify it. One of these processes is coagulation. Chemicals such as alum are added to the water. They form in water tiny fluffy masses rather like snowflakes. These attach themselves to the microscopic particles found in ordinary river water and carry them to the bottom of large sedimentation tanks.

From the sedimentation tanks the water passes through filter beds of fine sand. They remove any particles remaining in the water. Finally, chlorine is added to the water to kill any germs that might still be present. Other materials such as lime and char-coal may also be added during treatment. The charcoal, for example, removes traces of substances that cause unpleasant tastes or smells.

From the waterworks the now pure water is pumped by pumping station into the water mains which supply domestic and industrial users. In some small towns the pressure to force the water through the mains is provided by a water tower. Water is pumped into the tower, but flows from the tower under gravity.

Waterworks

Water treatment

Rain clouds

Dam

Impounding reservoir

Water evaporation from sea

River

Intake

Local reservoir

Outfall to river

Waterworks

Sewage works

Water evaporation from river

Pump

Homes

Well

Water main

Waste Water

Factories

Down the Drain

Each of us uses about 30 gallons (135 liters) of water a day. We call the waste water, which contains all kinds of waste matter, sewage.

piped from the house drains into larger pipes called main sewers, which take it to sewage treatment plants, or sewage works. It then goes through a series of

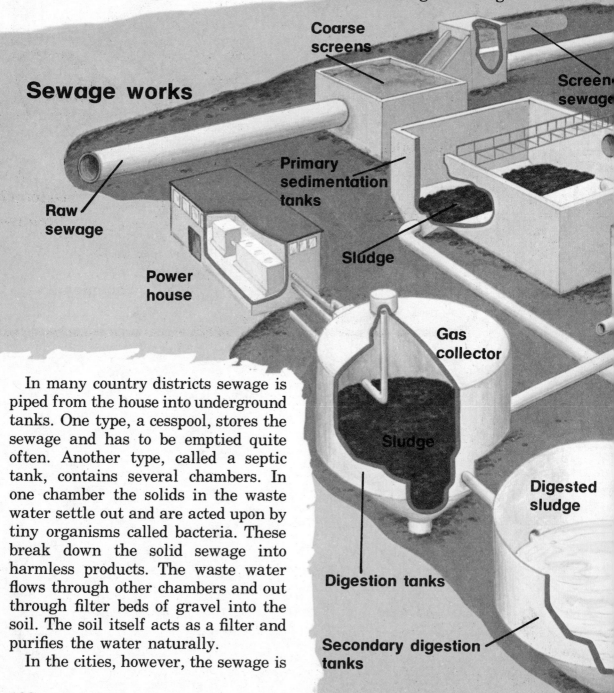

Sewage works

Coarse screens

Screen sewage

Primary sedimentation tanks

Raw sewage

Power house

Sludge

Gas collector

Sludge

Digested sludge

Digestion tanks

Secondary digestion tanks

In many country districts sewage is piped from the house into underground tanks. One type, a cesspool, stores the sewage and has to be emptied quite often. Another type, called a septic tank, contains several chambers. In one chamber the solids in the waste water settle out and are acted upon by tiny organisms called bacteria. These break down the solid sewage into harmless products. The waste water flows through other chambers and out through filter beds of gravel into the soil. The soil itself acts as a filter and purifies the water naturally.

In the cities, however, the sewage is

processes which convert it back into clean water. On entering the sewage plant, it first passes through coarse screens. The screens remove from the water such things as rag, newspapers and pieces of wood. Next the sewage passes slowly through channels and any grit in it settles out.

The grit-free sewage then goes into huge sedimentation tanks. Gradually the solid waste it contains sinks to the bottom to form a sludge. The water remaining, however, still contains traces of waste matter which must be removed. This is done by allowing bacteria to feed on it. In the plant shown below this happens in the aerator.

In some works this process is carried out by spraying the dirty water on to beds of gravel. After treatment in

Grit settling tanks

Grit free sewage

Grit

Aerator

Secondary sedimentation tanks

another sedimentation tank, the water goes back into the river.

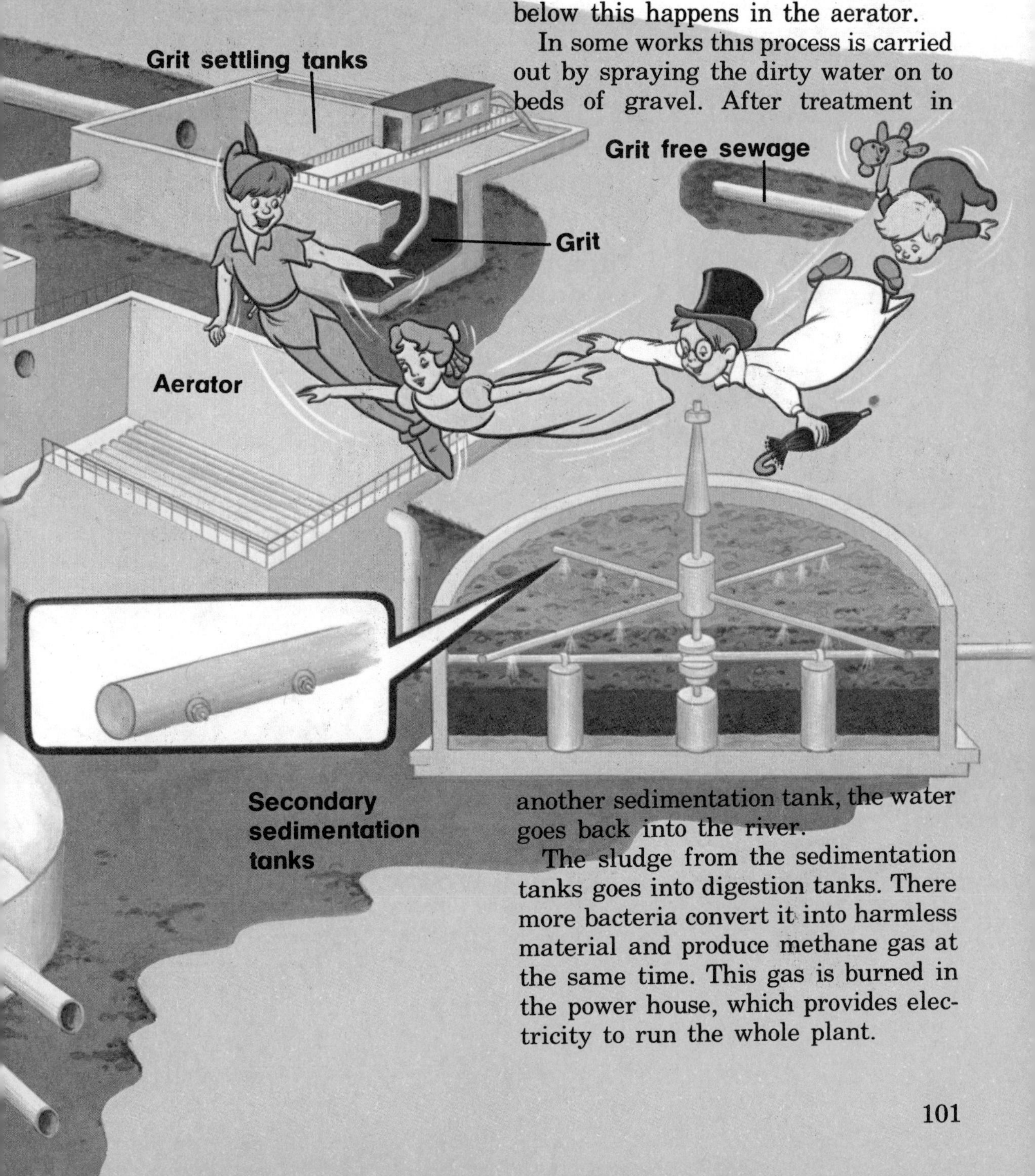

The sludge from the sedimentation tanks goes into digestion tanks. There more bacteria convert it into harmless material and produce methane gas at the same time. This gas is burned in the power house, which provides electricity to run the whole plant.

ndustries

In days long ago, country villages were to a large extent self-supporting. The people grew their own food, spun their own thread, wove their own cloth and made their own clothes. No village was without its forge, in which the blacksmith made and repaired farm implements, wagon wheels and the like, and shoed horses.

Today almost everywhere the things that were once made by hand are now made by machines, but in a few places the old ways remain. For example, in some parts of the world people still spin and weave cloth on hand spinning wheels and looms, and sell what they make. This is what is called a craft, or cottage industry. Other people practice similar crafts in their leisure time at home and at handicraft centers.

Spinning and Weaving

Most of the clothes we wear are made from cloth produced by machines in factories, but in some parts of the world cloth is still made by hand.

Spinning is carried out to make thread or yarn from wool, for example. Wool is made up of quite short fibers. In the spinning process the fibers have to be linked together and drawn out so that they overlap to form a continuous strand of yarn. In the simplest spinning process the person who spins holds a bundle of wool on a stick, called a distaff. With her fingers, she pulls out and lightly twists the fibers into a thread and winds it on another stick, or spindle, which she sets spinning like a top. As the spindle spins, it twists the thread into a strong yarn.

Most crafts people, however, now spin with a spinning wheel. It is a simple machine for turning the spindle and giving the thread a twist. The spinner turns a large wheel, which drives the spindle by means of a drive band and pulley.

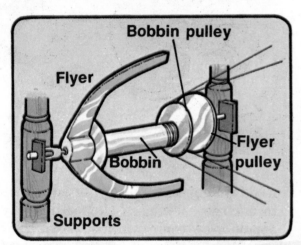

Bobbin pulley

Flyer

Bobbin

Flyer pulley

Supports

Driving band

Wheel

Spindle pulley

Head

Spindle

Bench

Support

Wool

After spinning comes weaving, which is done on a loom. In weaving, one set of yarns is threaded under and over another set of yarns, forming an interlacing criss-cross pattern. On a loom, one set of yarns (called the warp) stretches from the back to the front. Midway, the warp yarns pass through the eyelets of wires (heddles) held in two separate frames (harnesses). The frames are arranged so that one goes up as the other goes down. When this happens, a gap (shed) opens between different sets of yarns. It is through this gap that the cross-wise (weft) threads are carried in a shuttle.

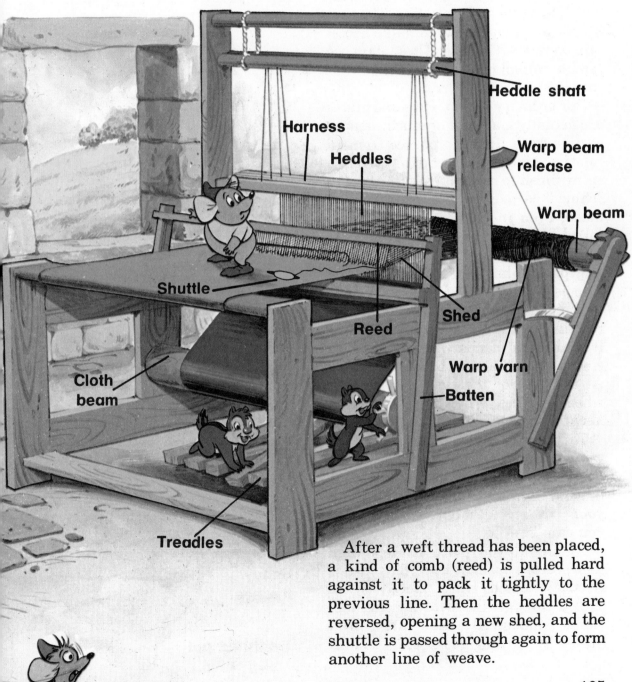

After a weft thread has been placed, a kind of comb (reed) is pulled hard against it to pack it tightly to the previous line. Then the heddles are reversed, opening a new shed, and the shuttle is passed through again to form another line of weave.

Pottering About

Most of the plates and cups and saucers we use in the home are made from special baked clay. They are forms of pottery. The finest pottery is porcelain, which is white and glass-like. The first people to discover how to make porcelain were the Chinese. These days we tend to call all our pottery "china," but this is not strictly correct.

Our ordinary "china" cups and plates are actually made out of much cheaper earthenware. This is produced from an inferior kind of clay but is given a shiny finish to make it look like proper "china." Almost all our pottery is made, even in industry, by a process called "throwing" on the potter's wheel. Throwing and making pottery is also a very popular hobby at craft centers and schools.

The potter's wheel is a turntable for rotating a lump of clay while you shape it with your hands. It is worked by electricity or, as here, by a foot treadle. At the base of the shaft driving this wheel is a heavy flywheel. This helps keep the shaft turning for a longer time.

To "throw" a pot, you place a lump of wet clay on the spinning wheel and push and pull it into shape with your fingers. You then carefully remove your "pot" and let it dry. When it dries, you can "fire" it.

To fire it, you place it in a high temperature oven, or kiln. This kiln is electric, heated when electricity is passed through the wire heating elements. Industrial kilns are often heated by burning gas or oil. The kiln

Potter's wheel

Water

Wheel

Shaping tools

Treadle

Heavy flywheel

Decorated pot

is lined with special refractory (heat resistant) bricks and insulating bricks. The temperature in the kiln varies from about 1,800°-2,100°F (1,000°-1,200°C).

After firing, the pottery is usually glazed and decorated. In glazing, the pottery is coated with a liquid called glaze and then fired again. The glaze melts into glass, giving the pottery a glassy coating and making it waterproof. The pottery may be decorated by painting either before or after glazing. It may also be decorated by transfers.

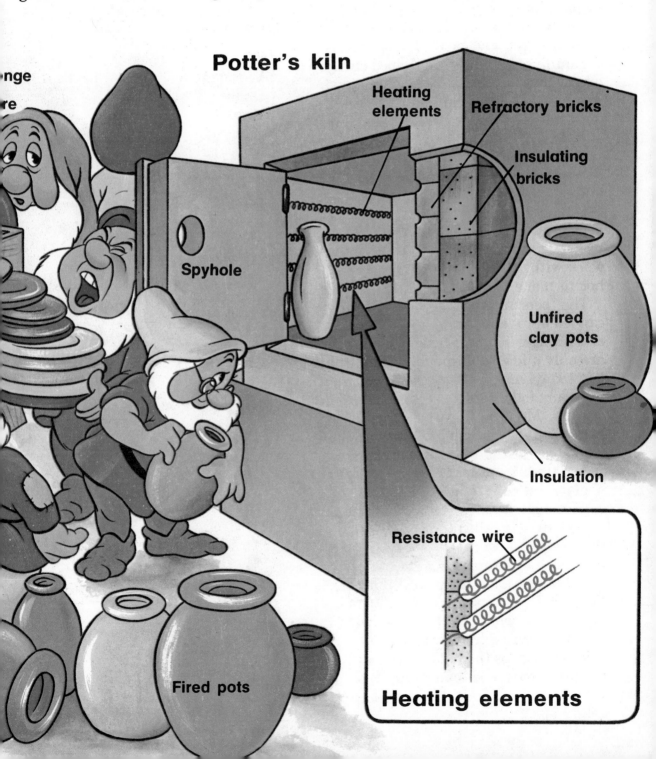

Potter's kiln

Heating elements

Refractory bricks

Insulating bricks

Spyhole

Unfired clay pots

Insulation

Resistance wire

Fired pots

Heating elements

Puff and Glow

Working with metals is another traditional craft that is still widely practiced. The people who do it are called smiths. Silversmiths and goldsmiths make fine works of art in the precious metals silver and gold. These metals are quite soft and can be shaped easily when they are cold by bending and hammering. They can also be drawn out into fine wire and beaten into thin sheets.

Most metals, however, cannot be shaped so easily. They are much harder and more brittle, which means that they tend to snap when stretched or bent too much. Our most useful metal, iron, is like this. To make it easier to work with, it first has to be heated red hot to make it softer.

The person who has traditionally carried out metalworking in the towns and villages is the blacksmith. There are only a few traditional blacksmiths left today, and most of them work at open-air folk museums and similar centers. Most of the work they once carried out is now done in engineering workshops using modern equipment.

The traditional blacksmith works in a place called a forge. The work he carries out – hammering red hot metal into shape – is called forging. He heats the metal he wants to shape, into a horseshoe for example, on the coals of a very hot fire, usually made of charcoal. To make the fire burn fiercely, the blacksmith works a bellows, which blows air through the coals.

He then grips the red hot iron with a pair of tongs and hammers it on a

Studded leather case

Bellows frame

Weighted upper ring

Draft nozzle

Fixed central ring

Flap valves

Lower pumping section

108

Blacksmith's forge

heavy iron anvil. The anvil has both flat and curved surfaces to help shaping and also a cutting edge. When the blacksmith wants to cool the iron, he plunges it into a trough of oil or water. Plunging it into oil, or "quenching" it, cools it more slowly than plunging it into water.

Chimney hood

Cutting tool

Hearth

Red hot horseshoe

Fixed cutter

Tongs

Hammer

Quenching trough

Anvil

Cooling trough

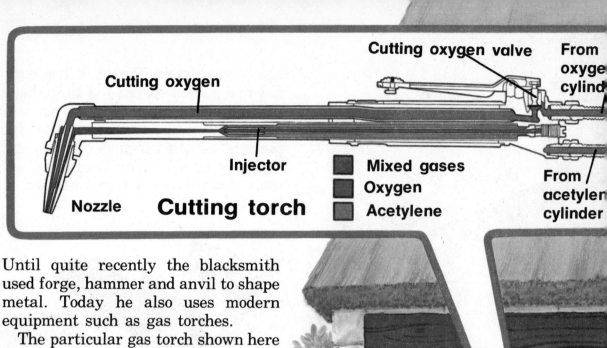

Cutting torch

Cutting oxygen

Cutting oxygen valve

From oxygen cylinder

Injector

Nozzle

- Mixed gases
- Oxygen
- Acetylene

From acetylene cylinder

Until quite recently the blacksmith used forge, hammer and anvil to shape metal. Today he also uses modern equipment such as gas torches.

The particular gas torch shown here is used for cutting metal. It uses the two gases, oxygen and acetylene, and is therefore called an oxyacetylene torch. The gases are kept under pressure in heavy iron cylinders and fed separately to the torch through flexible pipes. The gas pressures to the torch are adjusted by means of valves on the cylinders and are indicated on pressure gauges.

In the torch the oxygen and acetylene mix to form an inflammable mixture. This is then lit at the nozzle to produce an intensely hot flame, at a temperature of about 5,500°F (3,000°C). A channel in the center of the nozzle can deliver pure oxygen when the cutting valve is depressed. In operation, the oxyacetylene flame is directed on to the metal until this is red hot. Then a jet of oxygen is released through the nozzle on to the red hot area, which promptly burns away.

The gas torch is also used for welding operations. This time the cutting oxygen jet is not used. The ends of the two pieces of metal to be joined are heated red hot by the torch. Then extra metal is added to the joint from a so called filler rod. The red hot ends and the

Cartwheel

Bending, Jointing and Cutting

added metal flow together to form a solid bond.

Decorative wrought iron work is joined together by welding with a gas torch. Wrought iron is a form of iron which can be bent easily without cracking. The blacksmith bends iron strips into the shapes he needs and then welds them together inside a sturdier frame to make, in this picture, an attractive and personalized garden gate.

Pressure valves and gauges

Gas cylinders

Wrought iron gate

Anvil

Horseshoe

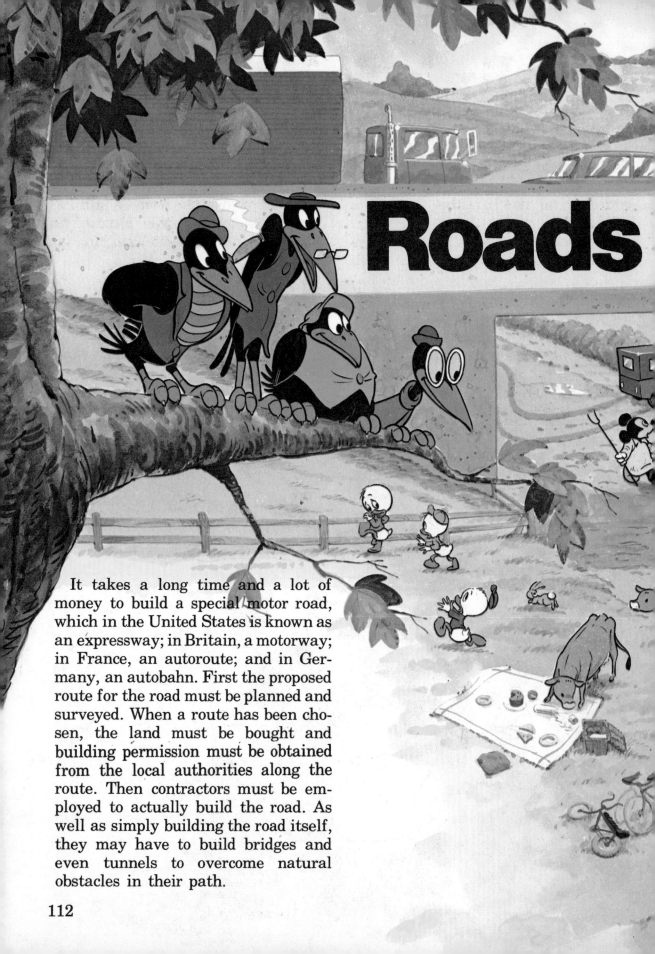

Roads

It takes a long time and a lot of money to build a special motor road, which in the United States is known as an expressway; in Britain, a motorway; in France, an autoroute; and in Germany, an autobahn. First the proposed route for the road must be planned and surveyed. When a route has been chosen, the land must be bought and building permission must be obtained from the local authorities along the route. Then contractors must be employed to actually build the road. As well as simply building the road itself, they may have to build bridges and even tunnels to overcome natural obstacles in their path.

Getting Started

Focusing sleeve

Circle reading eyepiece

Horizontal circle adjustment knob

Leveling screws

Altitude slow motion screw

Theodolite

Power shove

Surveyor

Telescope

Tripod

In the early stages of road building there is almost always a lot of earth to be moved.

These days road builders have heavy machinery to help them. They use powerful bulldozers to remove layers of soil, treestumps, rocks and the like. They are tractors with tough blades mounted at the front. The blade is mounted on a movable hydraulic boom, which works by liquid pressure. Power shovels are similar, but have scoops in the front.

scope on a tripod, but it is a more complicated instrument. It is mounted so that it can turn around horizontally on a base – the horizontal circle – marked with a scale of degree of angle. The surveyor uses this to measure the

Dump truck

Dumper truck

Making sure the road is straight and level and in the right position is the job of the engineers called surveyors.

They use the level to measure the height of distant points. It consists of a telescope mounted on a tripod. A "bubble level" attached to the instrument shows when the telescope is level – that is, parallel to the ground. The surveyor looks through the telescope at the scale on a measuring stick, or staff, held on the ground whose height is to be found.

The theodolite also consists of a tele-

angles between distant objects. He sights first one object through the telescope and takes one scale reading. He then swings the telescope around to sight the other object, and takes another scale reading. The difference between the readings gives the angle between the distant objects.

The surveyor can also measure the height, or altitude of distant objects. The telescope can seesaw up and down, again moving over a scale – the vertical circle. The surveyor sets up the instrument so that this scale reads zero when the telescope is level. He then sights a distant object through the telescope and notes the reading.

Excavating

Bulldozers are excellent for clearing surface vegetation and for removing relatively small amounts of earth, but other earth-moving equipment is needed as well.

Several kinds of excavators may be used, for example. One is shown here.

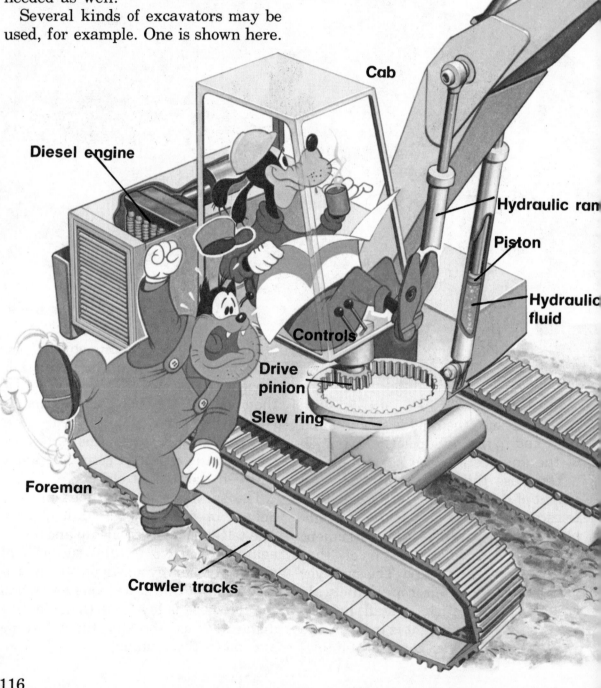

Hydraulic hose

Cab

Diesel engine

Hydraulic ram

Piston

Hydraulic fluid

Controls

Drive pinion

Slew ring

Foreman

Crawler tracks

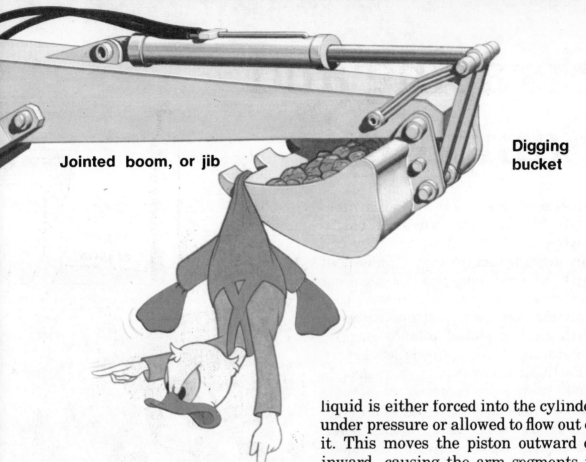

Jointed boom, or jib

Digging bucket

It works hydraulically, or by means of liquid pressure. Its lifting boom, or jib, is jointed, and hydraulic rams control the position of each joint and of the digging bucket. A ram consists of a cylinder and piston. In operation, liquid is either forced into the cylinder under pressure or allowed to flow out of it. This moves the piston outward or inward, causing the arm segments to rise or fall.

A hydraulic pump driven by the excavator engine supplies the liquid pressure required. The driver controls the flow of liquid into and out of the rams by means of valves. The excavator has its jib and control cab mounted on a turntable, or slew ring, so that it can turn around in any direction when excavating.

The engine also provides power to move the excavator backward and forward on caterpillar, or crawler, tracks. The tracks consist of endless belts of jointed steel plates. The excavator "lays" the tracks and then drives over them by means of toothed drive wheels. Track-laying vehicles like this can move more easily over soft ground than wheeled vehicles can. The tracks spread the load of the vehicle over a larger surface area.

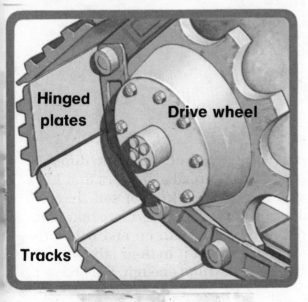

Hinged plates

Drive wheel

Tracks

117

Scraping and Sampling

Bulldozers (page 114) and excavators (page 116) are two kinds of earth-moving machines. However, they can only move or remove a small amount of earth at one time and they cannot really move it very far. In road construction, however, vast quantities of earth must be moved, often over quite a distance, as the route is leveled.

For bulk earth moving a scraper is used. It consists basically of a huge bowl on wheels. At its front lower edge is a tough steel cutting blade. When the scraper moves forward, the blade slices into the ground, and the slice of soil is forced into the scraper bowl.

The power needed for this operation is enormous, and most scrapers have twin diesel engines, one at the front and one at the rear. The engine at the front forms part of a tractor unit, which also carries the driver's cab. The tractor unit is linked to the rear bowl and engine unit by an articulated linkage. This linkage allows tractor and scraper unit to move independently from side to side for steering. It also allows the tractor and scraper units to roll independently when traveling over rough ground and prevents the tractor overturning if the scraper unit overturns. The scraper is emptied by tipping.

When the ground has been properly leveled, it must be made firm enough to support the road surface to be laid on it. Every kind of soil has different properties, so road engineers first have to find out what kind of soil they are dealing with. They therefore take samples of the soil both on and below the surface and test it in their laboratories. If it is not strong enough, they have to

Tractor

Front engine

Twin-engined scraper

Shock-absorbing hitch

Rear engine

Soil

Bowl

Blade

Bowl

Soil

Blade

mix other materials with it. Afterward they roll the surface over and over again to compact it, or make it firm. They roll it with massive steel rollers 10 feet (3 meters) or more in diameter, which are hauled by caterpillar, or crawler, tractors. Both smooth-surfaced rollers and sheepsfoot rollers are used. Sheepsfoot rollers have thick studs over their surface.

119

Wide wings for easier tipping by truck

Flow gates

Hopper

Variable speed conveyors

Hopper and feed

Tarmac

Hopper

Wide wings

Dump truck

Driver's seat

Screed

Laying the Surface

Once the ground has been accurately leveled and rolled firm, the road can be laid on it. The road is made up of not one but usually two or three layers. The base layers consist of crushed stone sometimes mixed with dry cement. They have an overall depth of from 1-2 feet (30-60 cm), depending on the strength of the underlying soil.

The top surface of most roads consists of a few inches of tarmac. Some roads though, are surfaced with concrete (see page 123). The word tarmac is short for tarmacadam, which is a mixture of crushed stone and tar (asphalt). It is named after one of the great pioneer roadbuilders, the Scot John Loudon Macadam, who constructed excellent roads from layers of crushed stones in the 1700s.

These days roads are laid by mechanical pavers like that shown in the picture. This machine is shown laying tarmac, but it can also lay crushed stone and dry concrete for the base layers. It has a working width of up to 26 feet (8 meters).

The paver moves slowly along, laying the tarmac in a continuous operation. A tip-up truck feeds tarmac into a hopper at the front. Twin conveyors on the floor of the hopper carry the tarmac through flow gates, into a screw conveyor, or auger. The auger distributes the tarmac left and right along the whole width of the machine.

The auger feeds the tarmac to the rear part of the paver, which is known as the screed. The screed lays the tarmac to the right depth and produces the right surface. It also vibrates and tamps (pounds) the tarmac to make it firm. The tarmac must be laid hot so that it flows more readily, and the screed is equipped with burners for this purpose.

The paver can be controlled and adjusted either from the driver's console at the front of the machine or from a control panel at the rear.

Conveyor carrying tarmac

Chain driven auger

Feed auger

Rolling and Concreting

In modern road building a mechanical paver lays the tarmac surface of the road (page 121). Immediately afterward, while the tarmac is still hot, a heavy road roller trundles back and forth over it. This heavy rolling compacts (firms) the tarmac and makes it into a watertight surface.

In the past the road rollers were powered by steam engines; now they are powered by diesel engines. They are usually "three-wheelers" like their predecessors, with the single front roller being used for steering. The rollers are made of steel and filled with water to make them very heavy. They are also sprinkled all the time with water to prevent the tarmac sticking to them.

For smaller rolling jobs, manually operated rollers are generally used.

The one shown here has twin rollers, but some models have a single roller. These rollers firm the ground or tarmac by rolling and vibration.

Engine

Handle

Fuel tank

Controls

Roller

Steering yoke

Vibrator roller

Front roller

Scraper bar

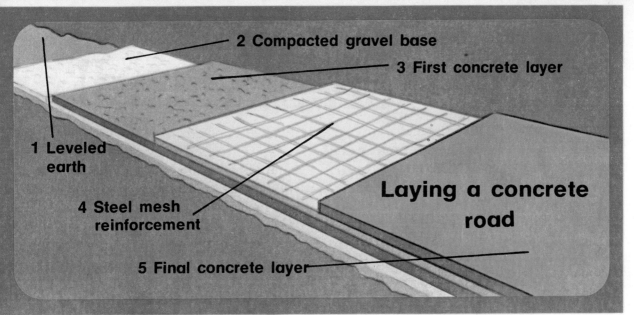

2 Compacted gravel base

3 First concrete layer

1 Leveled earth

4 Steel mesh reinforcement

Laying a concrete road

5 Final concrete layer

Enclosed cab

oad
ller

Scraper bar

Rear roller

Some roads are surfaced not with tarmac but with concrete. These days they are, like tarmac roads, laid by continuous paving machines. The paver is one of a number of machines which together form what is called the concrete "train."

A concrete road is built up layer by layer, as the diagram illustrates. First a layer of gravel is laid over the leveled ground and compacted. A concrete spreader puts down a layer of ready-mixed concrete, delivered to it by a mixer truck from a cement-mixing plant erected nearby. Following the spreader is a vibrator, which shakes the wet concrete to make sure it packs down firmly on the base.

On this layer of concrete goes a mesh of steel bars, which are included to give the concrete extra strength and reduce cracking. Then another layer of wet concrete is put down over the steel mesh. Following the spreader is another vibrator, again to pack the concrete down firmly. Finally the surface of the concrete is brushed to make it slightly rough. This is to provide better grip for car tires.

123

Road Works Ahead!

Often, when you see road work, you will see, and hear, the pneumatic drill.

The compressed air to power the drill is provided by a compressor which is driven by a gasoline or diesel engine. Some compressors use pistons to compress (squeeze) the air to high pressure. The one shown here has two tightly fitting vanes, which rotate in contact with each other in a figure-eight shaped cylinder. The vanes compress the air as they sweep swiftly around.

The compressed air is delivered by a rubber hose to the drill. The drill operator lets air into the drill by pulling the control lever. Then the drilling

Exhaust pipe

Radiator

Compressor

Plans

Air in

Drive gears

Vanes

Compressed air out

and hammering actions take place automatically. Inside the drill is a cylinder in which a piston is forced rapidly up and down by the compressed air. Each time it is forced down, it strikes the upper end of the drill bit and hammers it into the ground. The compressed air is channeled by automatic valves alternately above and below the piston through openings, or ports. After driving the piston, the air returns to the atmosphere through exhaust ports.

Pneumatic drill

Vibrator roller

Control knob

Valves

Upper inlet port

Cylinder

Piston

Exhaust ports

Lower inlet port

Air hose

Tool bit

Water main

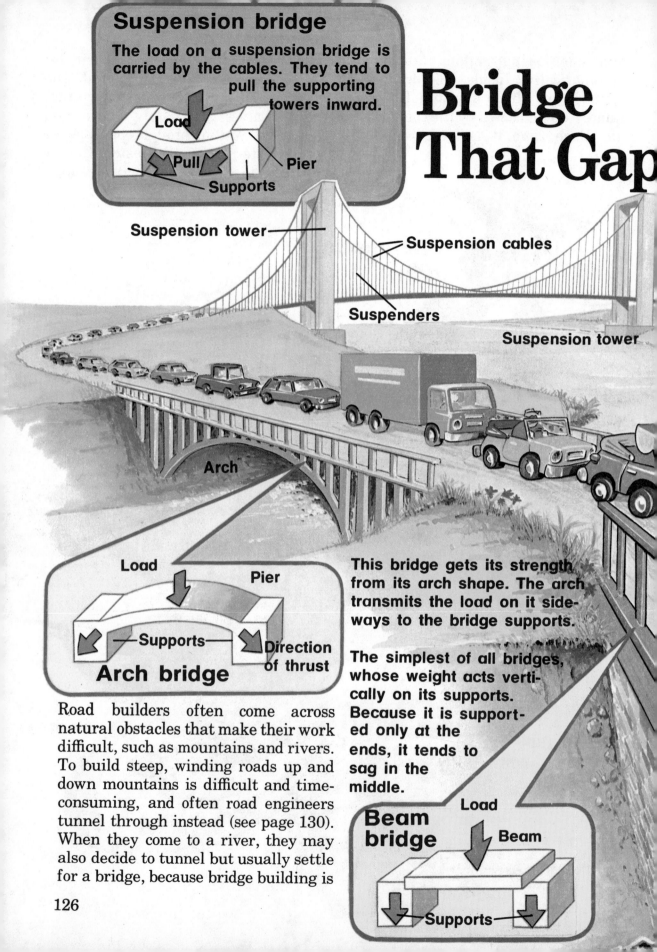

Suspension bridge

The load on a suspension bridge is carried by the cables. They tend to pull the supporting towers inward.

Load

Pull

Pier

Supports

Bridge That Gap

Suspension tower

Suspension cables

Suspenders

Suspension tower

Arch

Arch bridge

Load

Pier

Supports

Direction of thrust

This bridge gets its strength from its arch shape. The arch transmits the load on it sideways to the bridge supports.

The simplest of all bridges, whose weight acts vertically on its supports. Because it is supported only at the ends, it tends to sag in the middle.

Beam bridge

Load

Beam

Supports

Road builders often come across natural obstacles that make their work difficult, such as mountains and rivers. To build steep, winding roads up and down mountains is difficult and time-consuming, and often road engineers tunnel through instead (see page 130). When they come to a river, they may also decide to tunnel but usually settle for a bridge, because bridge building is much cheaper than tunneling.

If the river is quite shallow, a beam bridge is usually chosen. This is the simplest kind of bridge. It consists of a straight girder, or beam, supported at regular intervals underneath. The supports must be quite close together, otherwise the girders will sag in the middle.

If the river is wide and deep, an arch or suspension bridge will have to be built. The arch bridge may be made of steel girders, or with concrete reinforced with steel rods or cables. The suspension bridge has its deck hanging from steel cables, which are supported by tall steel suspension towers.

Bridge
deck

Moving Bridges

Sometimes the rivers to be bridged carry large boats and even ocean-going ships. Then the bridges either have to be built particularly high, which is very expensive, or they have to be designed to move out of the way of the passing river traffic.

There are several types of movable bridge. One is the swing bridge. This is often a simple girder bridge supported in the middle. It is mounted so that it can pivot about its support and swing around sideways.

Bridge operator

Girder trusses

Cen
pivo

The other movable bridge shown here is called the bascule. The bridge deck is divided into two halves, or leaves, which each pivot upward to allow boats to pass through. The leaves are counterbalanced for easier movement.

Another kind of vertically movable bridge has a bridge deck that moves vertically upward between two towers. It is called a vertical-lift bridge. There are even a few traveling bridges on which traffic is carried on a moving platform.

Counterbalanced opening leaves

Double bascule bridge

Counterbalanced opening leaves

Pivots

og mechanism

wing bridge

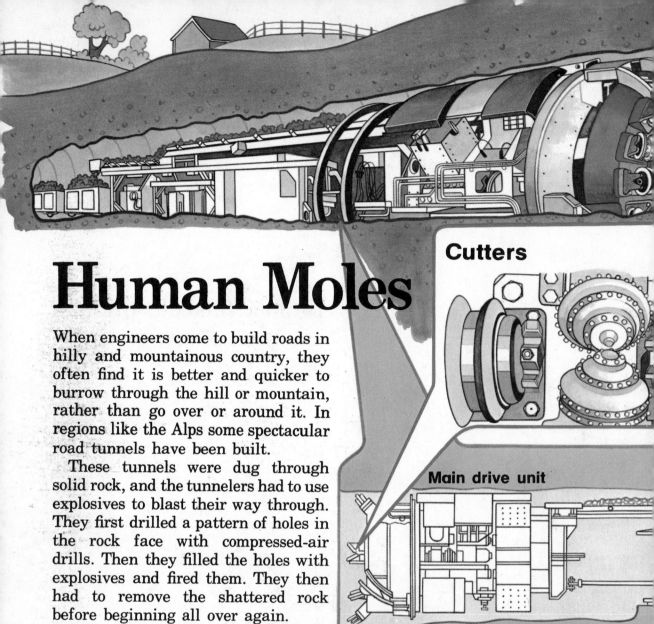

Cutters

Main drive unit

Cutting head

Human Moles

When engineers come to build roads in hilly and mountainous country, they often find it is better and quicker to burrow through the hill or mountain, rather than go over or around it. In regions like the Alps some spectacular road tunnels have been built.

These tunnels were dug through solid rock, and the tunnelers had to use explosives to blast their way through. They first drilled a pattern of holes in the rock face with compressed-air drills. Then they filled the holes with explosives and fired them. They then had to remove the shattered rock before beginning all over again.

This process takes a very long time, and in recent years tunnelers have started using tunneling machines to dig through rock. Tunneling machines have been used for a long time to dig through clay and soft ground.

One of the new rock-tunneling machines is shown here. This type is often called a "full-facer" or a "mole." It has a number of rotating wheels on the cutting head, studded with hard abrasive material. They grind their way through the rock face as they rotate.

In order to tunnel forward, the tunneling machine must anchor itself in some way. It does this by means of gripper arms which press outward against the sides of the newly bored tunnel. When the grippers are firmly fixed, the cutting head is thrust forward, and cutting begins. As the rock is cut, the pieces are picked up by a conveyor and carried to the back of the

Debris conveyor

Control cabin   Storage unit   Hydraulic unit   Switchgear unit

Tunneling machine

machine. There they fall on to another conveyor or into railroad cars and are carted away.

Tunneling in soft ground is easier because the cutting head can bore through more rapidly. The cutting edges can be simple knife blades. The trouble is that the tunnel tends to collapse as soon as it has been bored.

A soft ground tunneling machine must therefore have its cutting head protected by a shield, and it lines the tunnel as it goes along. It is often called a tunneling shield. In operation, the shield is forced ahead into the soft ground, pushing against the newly placed lining. The cutting head digs out the earth, and then a new section of lining is put in, and the process begins again.

The Leisurely Life

"All work and no play makes Jack a dull boy," goes the saying, and very true it is. Whatever kind of work we do, from time to time we need to have a rest from it. We need time to relax, time for leisure. If we don't take any time off, our work will eventually suffer, and so will our health.

One person's idea of "rest," or leisure, may be very different from another's. For some it means reading a book or lazing in the sun by a swimming pool with an ice-cold drink. For others it means doing something active, such as playing a sport, going hiking, gliding, mountain climbing or car racing.

You could hardly call these activities a rest, but they are a change from what the people normally do, and they know the truth of that other well-known saying: "A change is as good as a rest."

Going Camping

For those in need of something completely different, camping is popular.

To do things properly you will need pots and pans and a pressure stove, which uses kerosene. The kerosene is forced under pressure first through hot pipes and then into the burner. In the pipes it changes into a gas, which is then burned. The pipes have first to be heated by lighting methylated spirits beneath them.

Another popular stove is the gas stove, which works from a supply of "bottled gas." The gas is kept in the bottle under pressure, which makes it turn into a liquid. The liquid changes back into a gas when the pressure is released. The gas is then piped to a burner and lit.

Gas lamps are popular for camp lighting. As the gas burns, it makes a mantle glow white hot, and this provides the light. Kerosene lamps are also widely used. Their light comes from a burning wick, which dips into a tank of kerosene.

There is plenty of time when camping to take a quick nap or sunbathe. To prevent the sun's rays from burning you, you may need to rub some suntan cream on your skin. This contains a filter and helps screen your skin from the rays that burn.

To protect your eyes you will need a pair of sunglasses. The best ones have polarized lenses. This means they let through light rays vibrating in only one plane, say vertically or horizontally. Ordinary light waves vibrate in all planes.

Burner

Priming tray

Pressure pump

Filler

Air valve

Pressure stove

Kerosene tank

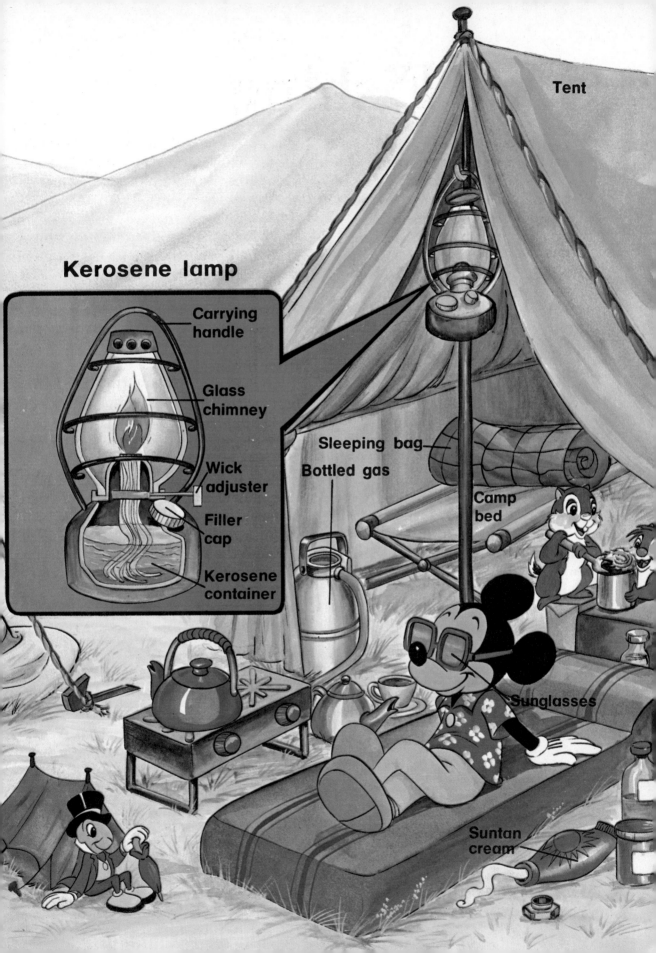

Tent

Kerosene lamp

Carrying handle

Glass chimney

Wick adjuster

Filler cap

Kerosene container

Sleeping bag

Bottled gas

Camp bed

Sunglasses

Suntan cream

Gone Fishing

One of the most peaceful pastimes in the countryside is fishing. Even if the fish are not biting very much, it is a pleasure just to sit quietly by the river, listening to the water gurgle by.

Many of us start our fishing, or angling, with a branch for a rod, a piece of string for a line, and a bent pin for a hook, but we soon swop this primitive equipment for proper fishing tackle. Fishing rods may be made from bamboo, fiberglass or even steel. The rod is fitted with wire eyelets along its length through which the line passes.

The fishing line these days is made of nylon yarn. It comes in various thicknesses and breaking strains (weights that will break it). The line is wound on a reel attached to the handle of the rod. A common kind of reel has a spool which winds up the line when you turn the winding handle. It may be a multiplying reel, which means that it is geared so that one turn of the winding handle turns the winding spool several times. The one shown here also has a guide which travels back and forth along the rotating spiral and causes the line to wind evenly on the spool.

The other main type of reel is the fixed-spool reel. In this reel the spool is stationary, and the line is wound on it by means of a metal arm ("flyer"). The flyer is attached to a drum, which rotates around the outside of the spool. For casting (throwing) the line, the flyer flips back and lets the line unwind from the spool.

Anglers may fish with a float and bait, with a fly, or with a lure. When fly-fishing, the angler casts the fly – a hook disguised as an insect – on to the surface of the water. He draws a hooked lure through the water. It may be a plug or a spinner. A plug is a kind of model fish. A spinner is a piece of metal which spins when it is pulled through the water. These lures resemble swimming fish and tempt predatory fish like pike to attack them.

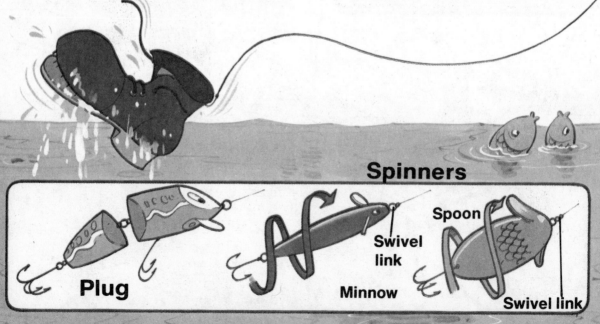

Spinners

Plug

Swivel link

Minnow

Spoon

Swivel link

Multiplying reel

Winding handle

Rod handle

Rotating spiral

Winding spool

Line

Rod

Line guide

Fixed-spool reel

Rotating drum

Fixed spool

Flyer flips back to release line

Winding handle

Moving flyer

Waterproof coat

Creel

Rubber boots

137

Sharp Shooting

Shooting, with hunting and fishing, has always been a traditional country activity, but these days it is carefully controlled so that wildlife is not threatened. People can still shoot as a sport, however, using clay discs as targets. This sport is known as clay-pigeon shooting or trapshooting. Trapshooting gets its name from the device that throws the clay targets into the air.

The trap has a pivoted arm which is attached to a spring at one end and holds the clay target at the other. To set the trap, the arm is pulled down, stretching the spring. When the trap is released, the spring causes the arm to

Thrower pulled back here

Propellant power

Wadded cartridge (for close shooting)

Shot

Shot

Percussion cap

Scatter shot cartridge

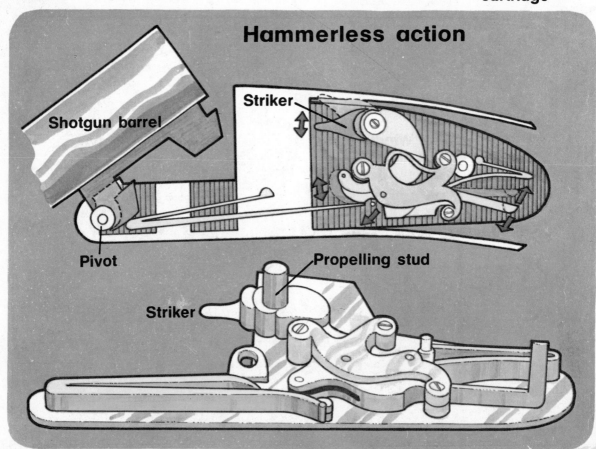

Hammerless action

Shotgun barrel

Striker

Pivot

Propelling stud

Striker

Spring release

Release position

Thrower arm

Target is placed here

Pivot

Trap

Clay target

Loading position

Shotgun

Gundog

arc upward and eject the target. The target itself is made of a mixture of pitch and clay. It is very brittle and shatters easily. The marksman is usually about 100 feet (30 meters) from the target when he hits (or misses!) it.

Marksmen fire shotguns in clay-pigeon shooting. The inside of the barrels of these guns is smooth and not grooved as it is in a rifle. The ammunition is a cartridge, which has a brass base, and a casing of thick waxed paper. In the middle of the base is a percussion cap, which is struck by a pin, or striker, when the trigger is pressed. The cap fires and explodes the powder which propels the pellets ("shot") from the cartridge and out of the barrel.

Most shotguns are double-barreled, with their barrels side by side. Older shotguns have sprung hammers which fire the cartridge when they are released by the triggers. Modern shotguns have a hammerless action like that shown here.

The size of a shotgun is measured in terms of the bore, or gauge, of its barrels. A 12-bore is the commonest size. This means that a lead ball weighing one-twelfth of a pound would just fit inside the barrel.

Racing Cars

If you are mad about engines, cars and speed, then car racing would suit you. The kind of car racing called rallying takes place on ordinary roads, using ordinary cars (see page 142), but most car races take place on special tracks, or circuits, away from ordinary roads.

The fastest and most exciting races are Grand Prix ("Grand Prix" means "big prize" in French.) Cars which take part in Grand Prix races are specially built and have little in common with a family car. An important United States race is The Indianapolis 500.

The Grand Prix car has a single-seat body and a very powerful engine, which may have three times as many cylinders as an ordinary car engine (four cylinders). The engine is usually made of aluminum, not iron, for lightness. Both engine and gearbox are placed behind the driver, and the oil tank and engine-cooling radiator are placed at the side. Air for the engine is scooped in by the air intake above the driver's head.

The body is very well streamlined so that it can "slip" through the air more easily. On some circuits the racing cars may speed at over 150 mph (250 km/h). They go so fast these days that they have aerofoils fitted at the front and back. These act in the opposite way to the wings on an airplane and press the car down on the ground. The very wide, smooth tires also help the car hold the road better.

Racing cars must also have powerful

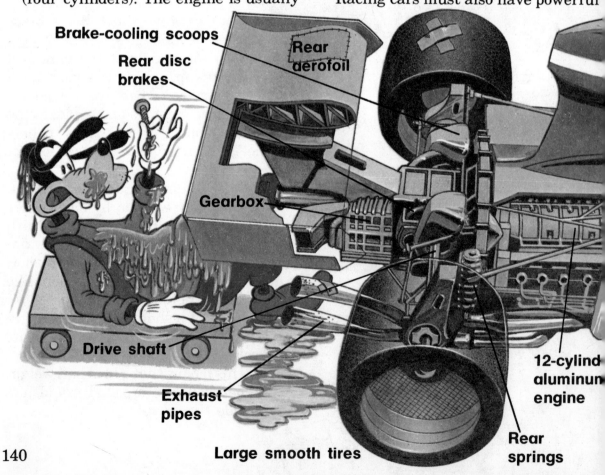

Brake-cooling scoops

Rear disc brakes

Rear aerofoil

Gearbox

Drive shaft

Exhaust pipes

Large smooth tires

12-cylinder aluminum engine

Rear springs

Dragster

brakes. They have four large disc brakes, two on the front wheels and two in the final drive at the rear. In case of accidents an anti-roll bar is fitted behind the driver's head so that he will be protected if the car rolls over.

A different kind of racing car is the dragster shown on the right. It has a huge engine mounted on a very long "skeleton" body. It is built purely for rapid acceleration over a short distance (usually about $\frac{1}{4}$-mile, 400 meters).

Grand prix racer

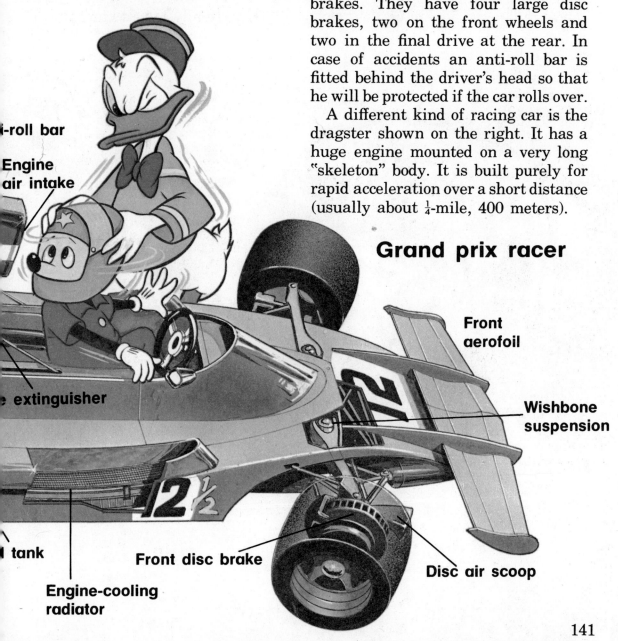

-roll bar

Engine
air intake

e extinguisher

Front
aerofoil

Wishbone
suspension

tank

Front disc brake

Disc air scoop

Engine-cooling
radiator

Rough Riding

There are other kinds of motor sport besides track racing. Rallying is one of them. Rallying is done with ordinary cars and takes place for much of the time on ordinary roads. There are several famous international car rallies, including the Monte Carlo Rally and the East African Safari Rally.

Local rallies are held in many areas of the United States. There are usually two people in each car – a driver and a navigator. The driver concentrates on driving, while the navigator reads the maps and plots the route they should take. Usually the rally team are given cryptic (disguised) clues as to where they should go and what they should do. They usually have to find the ans-

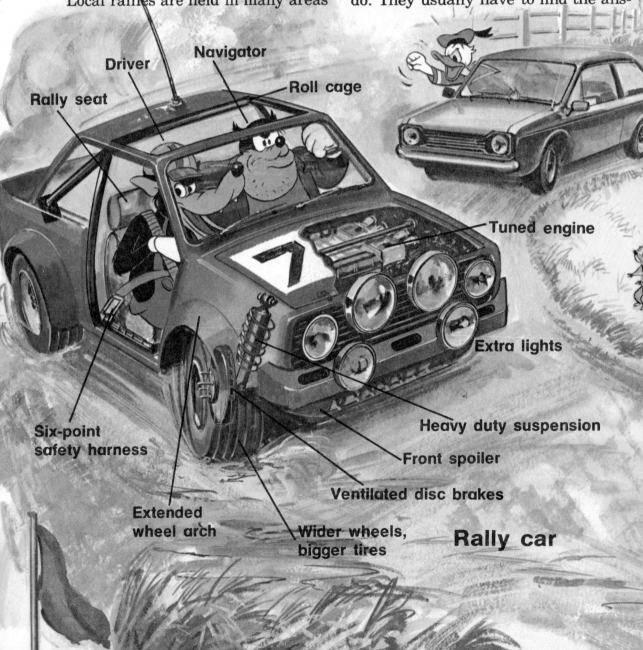

Driver

Navigator

Rally seat

Roll cage

Tuned engine

Extra lights

Six-point
safety harness

Heavy duty suspension

Front spoiler

Extended
wheel arch

Ventilated disc brakes

Wider wheels,
bigger tires

Rally car

wers to certain questions relating to objects along their route. For each correct answer they earn points. They may also be checked in at certain checkpoints, and may receive penalty points if they are late.

National and international rallies are much more demanding. Each car must keep to a specific schedule and to strict times. Special time trials are held at intervals throughout the rally over difficult courses, usually off the main roads. The cars used at these rallies are also special. They are basically the same models as you can buy, but they are specially prepared and have extra equipment to help them survive the punishment they will take during the rally.

The rally car in the picture shows many of these special features. It has a strengthened body so that it can roll on its roof without the passengers being

Scrambling bike

Uprated suspension

Chunky tires

Tuned engine

Higher ground clearance

crushed. It has tougher suspension and wider wheels to make it grip and ride more easily over rough ground. It also has bucket seats with a special safety harness. Its engine is highly tuned, or modified to give better acceleration and higher top speed. Its brakes may be ventilated so that it can slow down faster.

Two-wheel rough riding is also popular in the sport known as scrambling. The scrambling motorbike has a highly tuned engine, tougher suspension and chunky tires for extra grip. The frame of the bike is set higher off the ground than in normal bikes so that it can ride more easily over bumpy ground.

Tow plane

Rising
air currents

Hill

Up in the Clouds

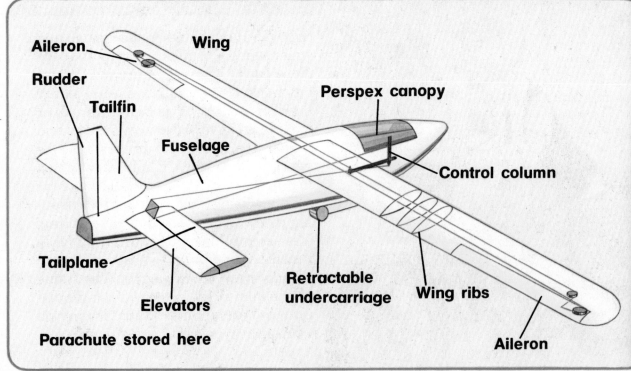

Aileron

Wing

Rudder

Tailfin

Perspex canopy

Fuselage

Control column

Tailplane

Retractable
undercarriage

Wing ribs

Elevators

Parachute stored here

Aileron

If motor racing is too noisy for you, perhaps you would prefer gliding instead. You soar like a bird high in the sky on currents of air. The plane you use is called a sailplane, or glider. It looks much like an ordinary airplane, but it is very much lighter and has much longer wings.

The main difference, however, is that a sailplane has no engine, and has to be launched into the air. Usually it is towed into the air by a light, powered plane. When the pilot has reached the required height, he unhooks the towline and starts to soar.

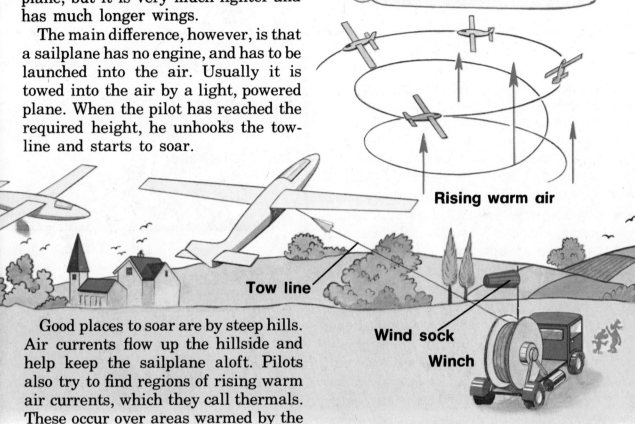

Cumulus cloud

Rising warm air

Tow line

Wind sock

Winch

Good places to soar are by steep hills. Air currents flow up the hillside and help keep the sailplane aloft. Pilots also try to find regions of rising warm air currents, which they call thermals. These occur over areas warmed by the sun and hot buildings. They are also found in the fluffy white clouds of summer, the cumulus clouds.

Sailplanes may also be ground-launched. This is usually done with a powerful winch. The tow line is attached to the sailplane at the end of a long runway, and the winch starts winding it in very rapidly. When the sailplane has reached take-off speed, it can get airborne. Sometimes a car is used instead of a winch for launching.

A typical sailplane has a body made out of lightweight materials such as plywood, fiberglass and aluminum.

Empty it may weigh only about 450-650 lb (200-300 kg), depending on its size. A sailplane is usually described by the span, or overall length, of its wings.

The sailplane has similar control surfaces to an airplane. It has ailerons on its wings, which move up and down to make the wings tilt. It has a rudder on the tailfin to make the plane point to the left or right, and it has elevators on the tailplane to make the nose point down or up. The pilot moves a combination of these control surfaces when he wishes to climb, dive and turn (bank) in the air.

Skiing

When it snows, the drab winter countryside is transformed into a sparkling white fairyland. The snow makes traveling more difficult, but provides the opportunity for many kinds of exciting winter sports, such as tobogganing and skiing, not to mention snowballing!

The most popular form of skiing is downhill skiing, with skiers hurtling down mountain slopes. They are carried to the top of the slopes by ski lifts. The one shown in the picture is a chair lift. Other lifts have a simpler arrangement, such as a T-bar, so called because it is like an upturned T (like this ⊥).

The skier wears strong, well-fitting boots which are clamped on to the skis. The clamping fixtures, or bindings, vary from ski to ski. The system shown here uses wires which are snapped tight around the boot when you pull the lever toward you. The bindings are designed so that they open automatically when the strain on them is too great, as might happen in a heavy fall.

The skis themselves are made usually of laminates (layers) of wood, plastic and metal. They are turned up at the front, and are typically about 3 inches (8 cm) wide and 7 feet (2 meters) long. Shorter skis are popular with beginners, and longer ones are used by ski jumpers, who launch themselves into the air from specially prepared slopes.

Ordinary vehicles are of little use for traveling over fresh snow, which is why the snowmobile was invented. The snowmobile has a small gasoline

Ski-boot fastening

Clamping lever

Spring

Boot

Ski

Fastening wire

Ski stick

Ski lift

engine which drives a single or double track at the rear, like a caterpillar track. The track spreads out the weight of the vehicle and driver over a large area and prevents it sinking into the snow.

The snowmobile is steered by handlebars, which move a pair of skis at the front. Speed is controlled by means of a throttle and brake on the handlebars.

Handlebars

Engine

Track

Fuel tank

Drive wheels

Steering skis

Snowmobile

On the Rack

The ski lifts (page 146) built to carry skiers up to the top of the ski slopes are quite a recent development, but their larger cousins, the aerial cablecars, have been in use in the mountains for many years. The cablecar, also called an aerial ropeway or téléphérique, can climb very steep slopes.

The "track" consists of a number of thick steel cables suspended high in the air from steel towers. The passenger car hangs by an arm from a trolley, which travels on wheels along the cables. One of the cables is actually attached to the trolley and pulls it and the passenger car along. A special braking system prevents the trolley getting out of control in an emergency.

Cablecars usually work in pairs on parallel cable "tracks" on what is called the funicular principle. This means

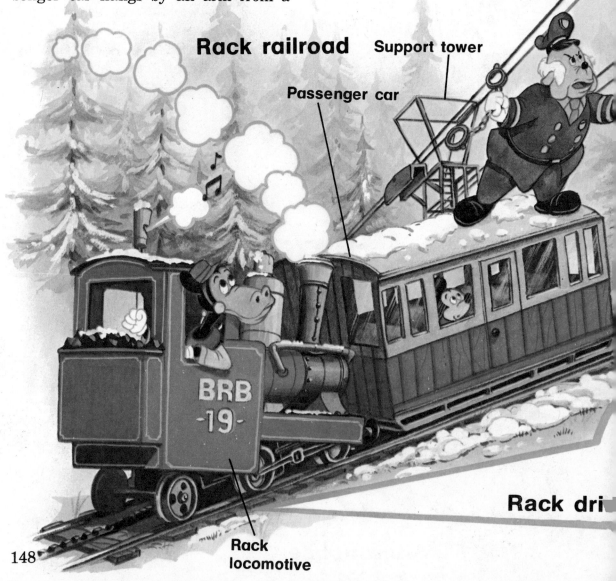

Cable 'track'

Rack railroad

Support tower

Passenger car

BRB -19-

Rack dri

Rack
locomotive

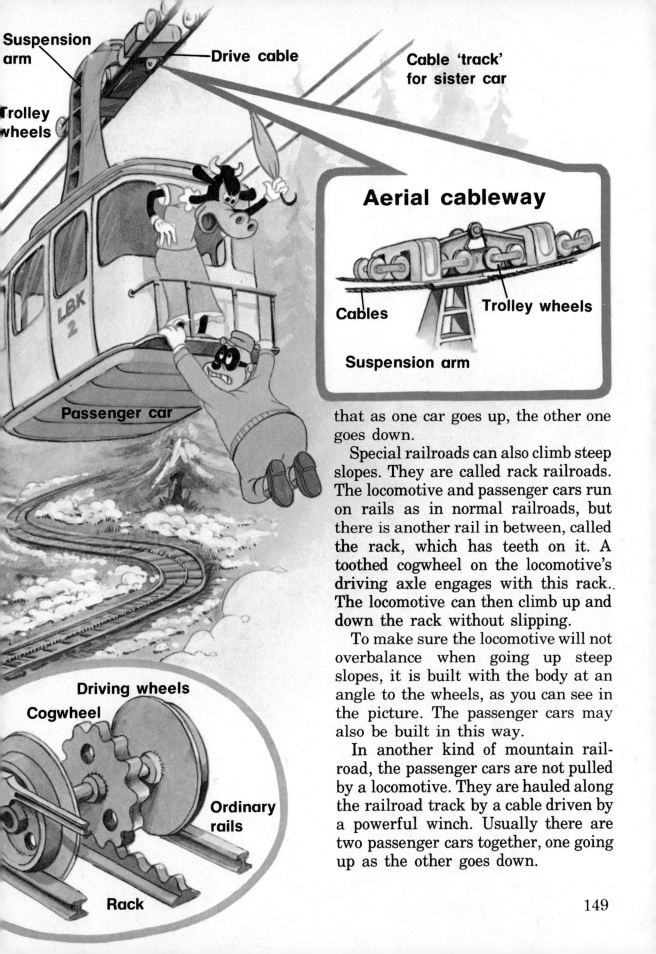

Suspension arm

Drive cable

Cable 'track' for sister car

Trolley wheels

Aerial cableway

Cables

Trolley wheels

Suspension arm

Passenger car

Driving wheels

Cogwheel

Ordinary rails

Rack

that as one car goes up, the other one goes down.

Special railroads can also climb steep slopes. They are called rack railroads. The locomotive and passenger cars run on rails as in normal railroads, but there is another rail in between, called the rack, which has teeth on it. A toothed cogwheel on the locomotive's driving axle engages with this rack. The locomotive can then climb up and down the rack without slipping.

To make sure the locomotive will not overbalance when going up steep slopes, it is built with the body at an angle to the wheels, as you can see in the picture. The passenger cars may also be built in this way.

In another kind of mountain railroad, the passenger cars are not pulled by a locomotive. They are hauled along the railroad track by a cable driven by a powerful winch. Usually there are two passenger cars together, one going up as the other goes down.

Radio-controlled Models

Making models of cars, boats and planes is one of the world's greatest hobbies. Modelers make their models from wood, plastic or metal.

The models can be powered by electric motors or tiny fuel-burning engines, and they can be operated and controlled at a distance by radio control. The operator has a transmitter which sends out radio waves to his model. Different waves, or channels, are used to operate various controls. The waves move the controls through tiny motors, or servos.

The simplest models to control are cars and boats. The model car shown

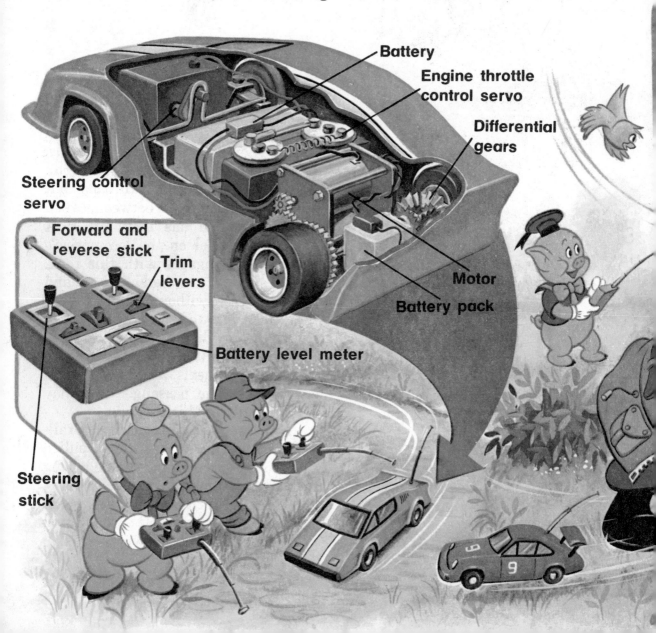

Battery

Engine throttle control servo

Differential gears

Steering control servo

Forward and reverse stick

Trim levers

Motor

Battery pack

Battery level meter

Steering stick

has an electric motor. It has two main controls, one for steering, the other for speed. The model boat has a tiny engine, whose speed is controlled by a throttle moved by radio signals. Different signals steer the boat by moving the rudder.

The trickiest model to build is an airplane that will actually fly. It must be carefully designed and perfectly balanced. Three or four controls are needed to make it fly any way you like.

They all need different radio channels. The model in the picture has controls to move the rudder on the tail fin and the elevators on the tailplane. Another controls the speed of the engine that spins the propeller. Many model planes also have controls for moving the ailerons – surfaces on the outer, rear edges of the wings. With radio control over rudder, elevators, ailerons and throttle, you can make your model plane perform all manner of aerobatics.

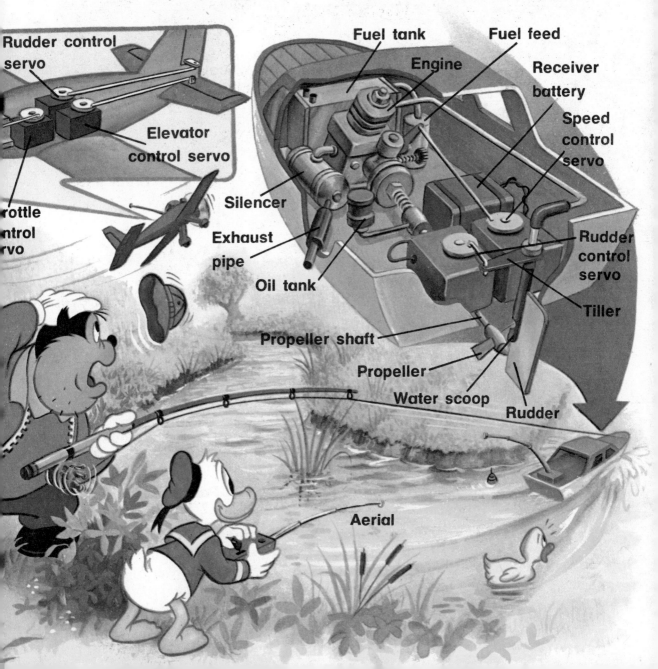

Rudder control servo

Elevator control servo

Throttle control servo

Fuel tank

Engine

Fuel feed

Receiver battery

Speed control servo

Silencer

Exhaust pipe

Oil tank

Rudder control servo

Tiller

Propeller shaft

Propeller

Water scoop

Rudder

Aerial

Telescope

Object lens

Erecting lenses

Light path

Inverted image

Focusing wheel rack and pinion

Erect image

Eye cup

Fixed eyepiece lenses

Reversing prisms

Path of light

Tripod

Object lens

152

Seeing Afar

If you are a birdwatcher, or naturalist, you often cannot get close enough to birds and animals to identify them or see what they are doing. Your eyes, however good they are, are just not powerful enough. The answer is to use a pair of binoculars.

Binoculars magnify, or enlarge the object you are viewing, and in effect take you much nearer to it. They are a form of compact telescope, and they took over from the telescope as a means of viewing distant objects. Telescopes are still used widely by astronomers for looking at the stars and planets. "Telescope" means seeing at a distance.

The simplest telescope has two lenses. One, the object lens, bends the light rays coming from an object to form an image. You then look at the image through another lens, called the eyepiece. The eyepiece magnifies, and you see a magnified image. To make the image sharp, you move the eyepiece tube in or out. This is called focusing.

In this simple telescope the image you see is upside-down. This does not matter if you use it for gazing at the stars, but if you want to use it for looking at objects on the ground, then you want the image to be the right way up. So ground, or terrestrial telescopes have an extra lens system inside them. It is called an erecting lens.

"Binocular" means "two eyes," and binoculars have viewing lenses for both eyes. They are really twin telescopes. Each half of the binoculars has an object lens and an eyepiece lens. The distance between them can be adjusted for focusing by moving an adjustment wheel. The wheel moves both halves of the binoculars together. Some binoculars have an adjustable eyepiece as well to allow for people having different eyesight in each eye.

Why are binoculars so much smaller than telescopes? The answer lies in specially shaped wedges of glass between the object and eyepiece lenses. They are glass prisms, placed so that they reflect the light rays passing through several times. They, as it were, "fold" the path of light. This allows the object and eyepiece lenses to be brought closer together.

eyepiece

Binoculars

Focus adjustment wheel

Adjustable eyepiece

Width adjustment

Index